FORWARD!

Student Book

2

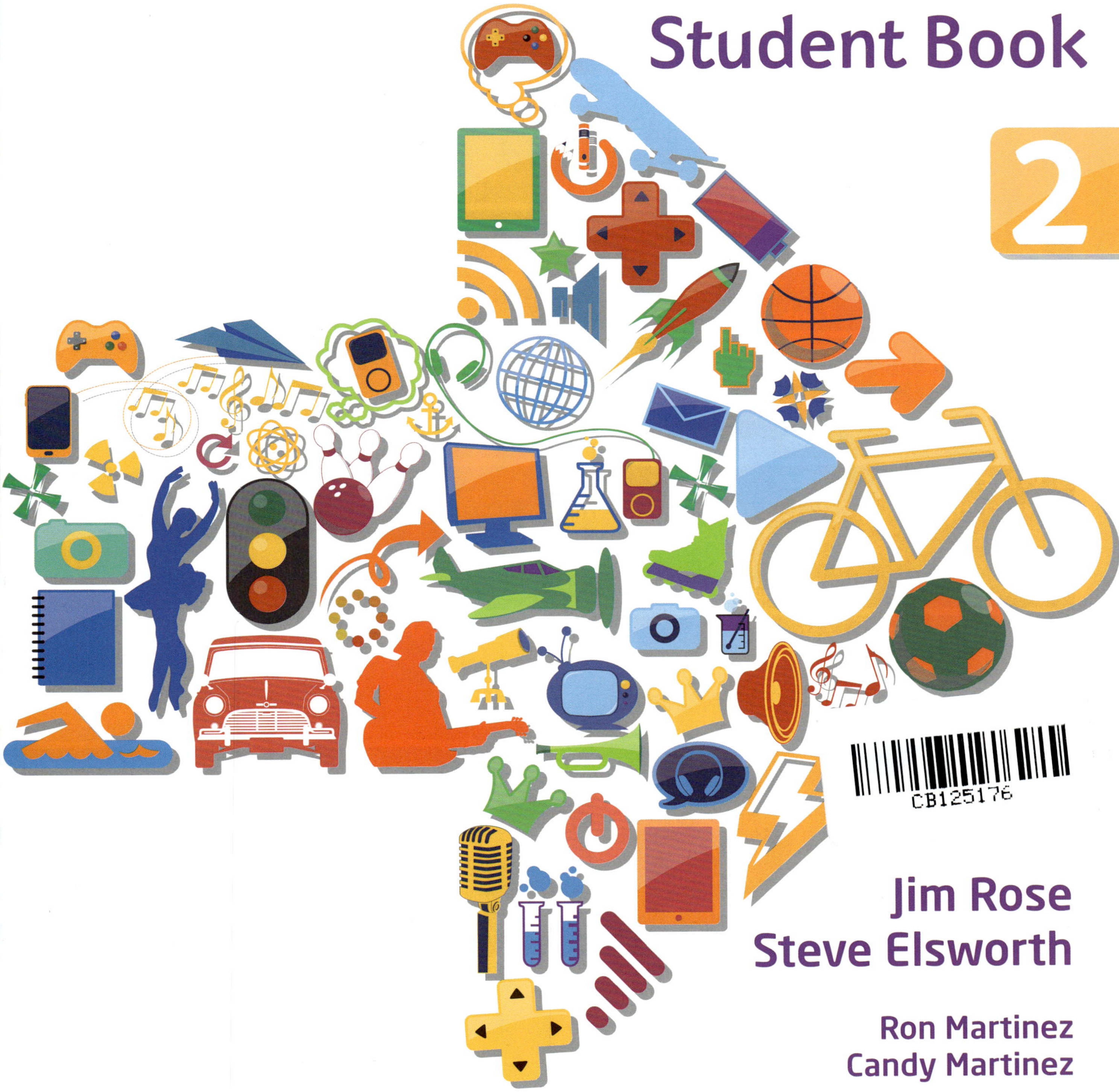

Jim Rose
Steve Elsworth

Ron Martinez
Candy Martinez

Contents

Starter

1 **Complete the missing parts.**

2 **Write the correct possessive adjectives.**

1 Joe, are these _your_ CDs?
2 This is Mark. Frank is ______ dad.
3 This is Ellie. Frank is ______ dad.
4 Mark, is Ellie ______ sister?
5 My parents are called Jenny and Frank. Jenny's Café is ______ café.
6 Hi, ______ name's Martina. I'm Italian.
7 Mark and Ellie are in the kitchen with ______ mom.

Possessive adjectives

Singular		Plural	
I	my	we	our
you	your	you	your
he	his	they	their
she	her		
it	its		

3 Write *this* or *that* in the sentences.

1 ___*This*___ is my bag.

2 ________ is my computer.

3 ________ is my puppy.

4 ________ is my notebook.

5 ________ is my sister.

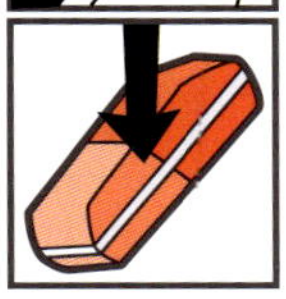

6 ________ is my eraser.

4 Write *these* or *those*.

1 ___*These*___ are my books.

2 __________ are my parents.

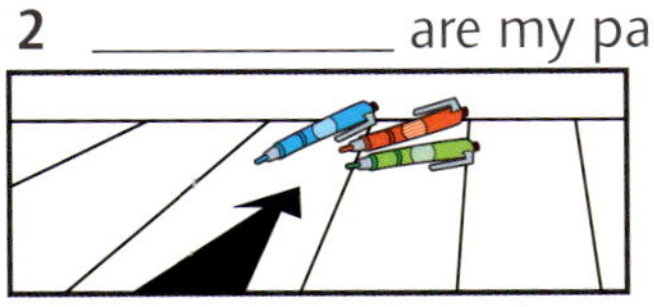

3 __________ aren't my pens.

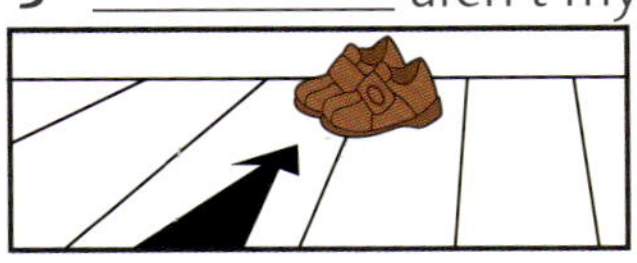

4 Are __________ your shoes?

5 __________ are my friends.

5 Complete the text with *am*, *is* or *are*.

Johnny Depp and Keira Knightley [1] ___*are*___ actors. They [2] ________ in the movie *The Pirates of the Caribbean*. "I [3] ________ Captain Jack Sparrow in the film and Keira [4] ________ Elizabeth Swann. We [5] ________ friends too." Johnny is American. Keira is from England.

6 Write the correct negative forms.

1 Johnny Depp is an actor. He ___*isn't*___ English.
2 Keira ________ from Los Angeles. She's from London.
3 Johnny ________ Willy Wonka in *The Pirates of the Caribbean* – he's Jack Sparrow.
4 Johnny and Keira ______ in *Star Wars*.

Language

Numbers

7 **Say these numbers round the class.**

20 19 18 17 16 15 14 13
12 11 10 9 8 7 6 5 4
3 2 1 ZERO!

8 **Match the numbers and the words.**

30 40 50 60 70 80 90 100

forty thirty fifty eighty ninety a hundred
seventy sixty

9 **Listen and write the numbers.**

a) *6* b) ______ c) ______ d) ______ e) ______
f) ______ g) ______ h) ______ i) ______ j) ______

10 **Write these numbers.**

42	*forty-two*	54	______	28	______
37	______	61	______	73	______
79	______	115	______	101	______

The alphabet

11 **Listen and repeat. Then say the alphabet round the class.**

A B C D E F G H I J
K L M N O P Q R S
T U V W X Y Z

12 **In pairs, practice spelling the numbers 0 – 100.**

A: How do you spell 58?
B: F – I – F – T – Y – E – I – G – H – T.

Days of the week

13 Complete the diary. Listen, check and repeat the days.

FEBRUARY

Mo ________	Weekend
Tu ________	Sa ________
We ________	Su ________
Th ________	*Notes*
Fr ________	

Saturday
Wednesday
Monday
Thursday
Sunday
Friday
Tuesday

Weather

14 What's the weather like? Match the sentences with the pictures.

1 

2 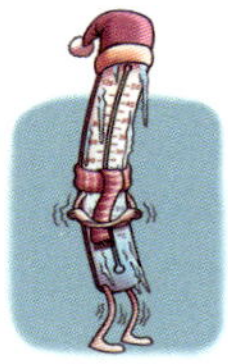

3 

4 

It's cloudy.
It's cold.
It's cool.
It's hot.
It's rainy.
It's sunny.
It's warm.
It's windy.

5 

6 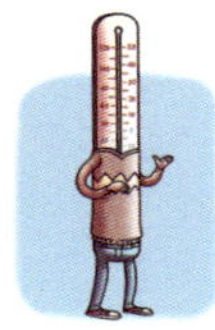

7 

8 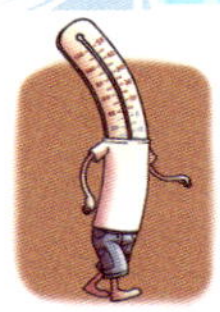

Colors

15 Match the colors with the words.

1 

2 

3 

4 

5 

6 

7 

8 

9 

10 

11 

black
blue
brown
green
grey
orange
pink
purple
red
white
yellow

1 Hi!

Presentation

1 Listen and read.

Expressions

- Excuse me.
- That's right.
- Wow!
- Welcome.

Airline Representative	Excuse me. Are you Joe?
Joe	Yes.
Airline Representative	Joe Murray?
Joe	Yes, that's right.
Airline Representative	Hi, Joe. How are you? I'm Cynthia. Is that your bag?
Joe	No, my bag is under my seat.
Airline Representative	OK. Please come with me.
Airline Representative	Wow, this is heavy! What's in here?
Joe	Some of my favorite things: my skateboard, some books, magazines, a video game, an umbrella, my laptop, some snacks…
Airline Representative	Wow… OK. So, where are you from, Joe?
Joe	I'm from Pretoria.
Airline Representative	Pretoria? Where is that?
Joe	It's a city in South Africa.
Airline Representative	South Africa… wow. Is this your first time in New York?
Joe	Yes, it is.
Airline Representative	Welcome to my hometown!
Joe	Oh, a New Yorker! I'm a Yankees fan.
Airline Representative	Yay, go Yankees! So… How old are you, Joe?
Joe	I'm twelve. How old are you?
Airline Representative	That's a secret!

Comprehension

2 Complete the information about Joe.

1 His name is __________.
2 His last name is __________.
3 He is ______________ (age).
4 His _________ is heavy.

Vocabulary

3 Match the words with the pictures. Listen, check and repeat the words.

A

B

C

skateboard
video game
book
snack
apple (A)
umbrella
laptop
magazine
cell phone

D

E

F

G

H

I

Pronunciation

4 Listen and repeat the words.

1 **cell** phone
2 **lap**top
3 **skate**board
4 **vid**eo game
5 book
6 snack

Speaking

5 In pairs, talk about the things in exercise 3.

A: *What's this/that?*
B: *It's a/an* _________.

1 Language

to be – questions and short answers

Am I ten?	Yes, I am./No, I'm not.
Is he/she/it American?	Yes, he is./No, he isn't.
Are we/you/they American?	Yes, we are./No, they aren't.

1 Make questions from the sentences.

1 You are from Canada.
2 You are from Rio de Janeiro.
3 She is a student.
4 I am twelve.
5 Joe is from South Africa.
6 This is from Paraguay.
7 It's a skateboard.
8 She's ten.
9 That's your bag.

2 Write the questions in the correct order.

1 you/ten/are?

____

2 Clyde/a/is/puppy?

____

3 are/student/a/you?

____

4 she/from/South Africa/is?

____

5 he/New York/from/is?

____

6 cell phone/this/is/a?

____

7 twelve/Mark/is?

____

8 San Francisco/from/is/Liz?

____

9 Rio de Janeiro/are/from/you?

____

Wh- questions

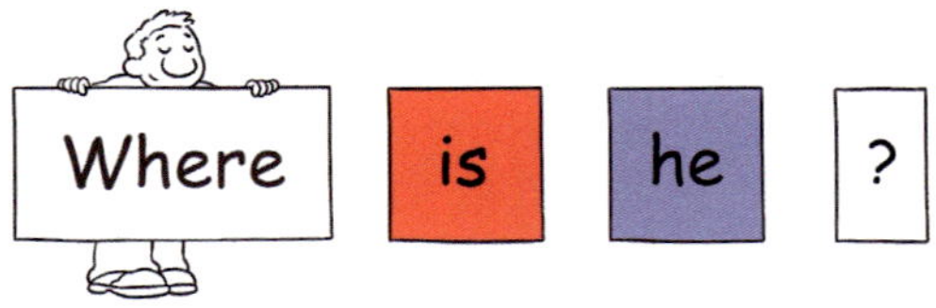

3 Write wh- questions.

1 How old/she?
2 Where/you from?
3 Where/that?
4 How old/you?
5 Where/he from?
6 What/your name?
7 What/your last name?

4 Ask and answer about the people.

A: *How old is Emma Watson?*
B: *She's… .*
A: *Where's she from?*
B: *She's from … .*

Emma Watson, 1990
Britain

Lionel Messi, 1987
Argentina

Will Smith, 1968
The USA

Shakira, 1977
Colombia

5 Write the questions about Cynthia.

A: 1 ______________________?
B: Cynthia.
A: 2 ______________________?
B: DiGiulio.
A: 3 ______________________?
B: New York.
A: 4 ______________________?
B: At the airport.
A: 5 ______________________?
B: It's a secret.

6 Listen and check your answers.

7 In pairs, ask and answer about your best friend.

What's his/her first name?

Rose.

8 Complete the table with the missing words.

Subject pronoun	Possessive adjectives
I	
	your
He	
	her
	its
We	
	their

9 Write the correct word.

1 (I) ___My___ friend is fifteen.
2 (She) ________ name is Cynthia.
3 (We) ________ teacher is from Brazil.
4 (You) ________ bag is heavy.
5 (He) ________ hometown is Pretoria.
6 (They) ________ favorite team is the New York Yankees.

Extra

10 Complete the information in the table.

	Me	Friend 1	Friend 2	The teacher
Name				
Age				
Hometown				
Favorite thing				

11 Use the information in exercise 10 to write sentences.

(I) My name is ______________________,
and I'm ______________________.
I'm from ______________________,
and my favorite thing is ______________________.
(friend) ______________________
name is ______________________,
and ______________________
is ______________________.
____
is from ______________________,
and ______________________
favorite thing is ______________________.
(teacher) ______________________
name is ______________________,
and ______________________
is ______________________.
____
is from______________________,
and ______________________
favorite thing is ______________________.

1 Language

+ *a/an* and *some* – singular and plural nouns

Countable nouns can be singular or plural.
Use *some* with plurals.

I have **a** chip.
I have **some** chips.

Uncountable nouns can't be plural.

I have **some** sugar.

Use *some* to describe a group of objects or people.

I have **a** magazine.

I have **some** magazines.

Finally in New York

12 Write *some* or *a/an*.

1 There ___are___ ___some___ clothes.
2 There ___is___ ___a___ laptop.
3 There ______ ______ books.
4 There ______ ______ snacks.
5 There ______ ______ videogame.
6 There ______ ______ cell phone.
7 There ______ ______ magazines.
8 There ______ ______ skateboard.
9 There ______ ______ umbrella.

13 **How many objects can you remember? In pairs, test your classmate.**

A (book closed): *There is a cell phone, a laptop, some magazines…*

B (book open): *Yes, that's right.*

Compete for who remembers more objects.

14 **Look at Joe's travel checklist. Compare it with the objects in your school bag.**

Things to take to New York	*My bag*
√ Passport	
√ Itinerary	
√ Laptop	
√ Cell phone	
√ Magazines	
√ Coat	
√ Videogame	
√ Snacks	
√ Skateboard	
√ Books	

15 **Use the information in exercise 14 to write sentences.**

There is a/an ______ in my bag.
There are some ______ in my bag.

1 Communicate

Vocabulary

1 Match the pictures to the words. Listen, check and repeat the words.

keys Ⓑ
toothbrush
sunglasses
wallet
clothes
mirror
hair brush
shoes

A

B

C

D

E
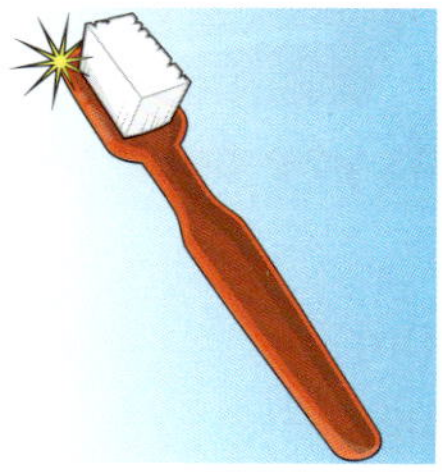

F

G

H

2 Cynthia is at the airport. She can't find her bag. Listen and check the objects in her bag.

Lost and Found (airport)

cell phone
clothes
hair brush
keys
magazines
mirror
passport
shoes
sunglasses
toothbrush
wallet

3 In pairs, A, you are the Clerk. Ask about his/her bag. B, you can't find your bag. Describe it.

A: *What color is your bag?*
B: *It's blue and red!*
A: *What's in it?*
B: *There's a/an... There are some...*

1 Skills

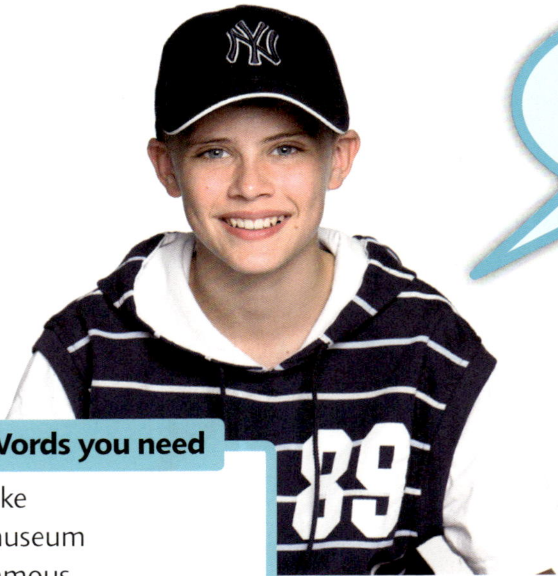

This is New York. It's my first time here and I love it! These are my favorite places in New York

Words you need

lake
museum
famous
delicious
gigantic

Reading

1 Match the photos with the captions.

1 Yankee Stadium – Baseball is my favorite sport and my team is the New York Yankees. This is the Yankee Stadium. It is really cool!!!
2 MoMA – This is a picture of MoMA, the Museum of Modern Art. It is in Manhattan.
3 This is Central Park. It's fun! There's a nice lake here.
4 The Statue of Liberty is really famous! It's gigantic, and you can go to the top!
5 This is Times Square. You can go shopping here and eat a delicious hot dog!

Listening

2 Listen to the radio report. Match the places to the descriptions.

Place	Description
Times Square	gigantic
Central Park	famous
Yankee Stadium	fun
MoMA	beautiful
Statue of Liberty	cool

Speaking

3 Write the names of your favorite places in your hometown. Also write a description. You can use some of the words below.

famous beautiful cool
gigantic fun nice interesting

Place	Name	Description
Square		
Park		
Stadium		
Museum		
Monument		

4 In pairs, ask and answer the questions.

A: *What's your favorite...?*
B: *My favorite (place) is (name). It's (description).*

Writing

Punctuation (1)

Useful punctuation marks for writing:

.	full stop
?	question mark
!	exclamation mark
he's	apostrophe
,	comma

5 Look at this page, and page 14. Circle 2 examples of each type of punctuation.

My favorite places

6 Write about you.

Research
Draw pictures or take photos to add to your description.

Draft
Write a draft.

My hometown is...
Here are some of my favorite places

Check
Check your draft – is the punctuation correct? Write the final version.

1 Look again

Language

1 Write the questions.

1 you/twelve/are?
Are you twelve?
2 Fluffy/a/is/dog?
3 are/teacher/a/you?
4 she/from/Argentina/is?
5 he/Paris/from/is?
6 wallet/this/is/a?
7 fifteen/Mario/is?
8 Tokyo/from/is/Ana?
9 Mexico City/are/from/you?

2 Write wh- questions.

1 How old/he?
How old is he?
2 Where/she from?
3 Where/that?
4 How old/you?
5 Where/he from?
6 What/their names?
7 What/your first name?

3 Write *some* or *a/an*.

1 There ________ ________ wallet.
2 There ________ ________ clothes.
3 There ________ ________ mirror.
4 There ________ ________ shoes.
5 There ________ ________ videogame.
6 There ________ ________ passport.
7 There ________ ________ books.
8 There ________ ________ toothbrush.
9 There ________ ________ apple

Vocabulary

4 Complete the words.

1 l __ __ t __ p
2 c __ __ l __ __ __ n e
3 m __ __ __ z __ __ e
4 u __ __ __ e l __ a
5 s n __ __ k

5 Write the words.

1. *mirror* 2. ____________

3. ____________ 4. ____________

5. ____________ 6. ____________

Communication

6 Write the answers.

1 Where are you from?
I'm from Brazil.
2 How old are you?
3 What's your favorite park in your hometown?
4 What color is your bag?
5 What's in your bag?

Now you can…	☹ 😐 ☺
use the verb *to be* in yes/no questions (*ex 1*)	
use the verb *to be* in *wh- questions* (*ex 2*)	
use *a, an, some* (*ex 3*)	
name everyday objects (*ex 4*)	
answer questions (*ex 6*)	

Game

Follow these instructions:

- Use a die to move.
- In each square, follow the instruction or answer the question. If you are not correct, you go back one square.

2 You can sleep in my room!

Presentation

1 Listen and read.

Ellie	Welcome to our house, Joe!
Mark	You can sleep in my room!
Joe	Cool – thanks! Wow, this is a big house.
Ellie	There are thirteen rooms. That's the living room.
Joe	Where's your room, Mark? Can I take my things there?
Mark	Sure. My room is upstairs. Come on!
Joe	Where can I put my things?
Mark	Under the bed is fine – or you can put it in the closet.
Joe	Do you like to play video games?
Mark	Of course! But the video game is in my sister's room.
Joe	Where's your sister's room?
Mark	It's next to the bathroom.
Mom	Kids! Lunch is ready!

Expressions

- Welcome
- Sure!
- Come on!
- Of course!

Comprehension

2 Complete the sentences with the correct words.

1 There are __________ rooms in Mark's house.
2 Mark's room is __________.
3 Joe can put his things __________ Mark's bed or __________ the closet.
4 Ellie is Mark's __________.
5 Ellie's room is __________ the bathroom.

Vocabulary

3 Match the rooms and furniture you can see in the house. Listen, check and repeat the words.

Rooms
bathroom (B)
bedroom
dining room
hall
kitchen
living room

Furniture
bed (3)
chair
stove
cupboard
desk
fridge
lamp
picture
sofa

Learning Tip
Storing vocabulary
Draw pictures to remind you.

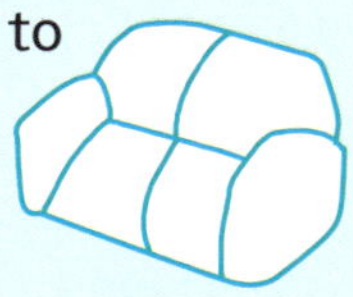

4 In pairs, ask and answer questions to guess the room.

B: *What's in the room?*
A: *A sofa and a TV.*
B: *Is it the living room?*

5 Write a sentence for each picture.

in on under next to
in front of behind

1 The bug's _*in*_ the box.

Game

6 Draw a bug in the house in exercise 3. In pairs, ask and answer.

A: *Where's the bug?*
B: *Is it on the table?*
A: *Yes, it is./No, it isn't.*

2 Language

+ *There is/There are* – affirmative

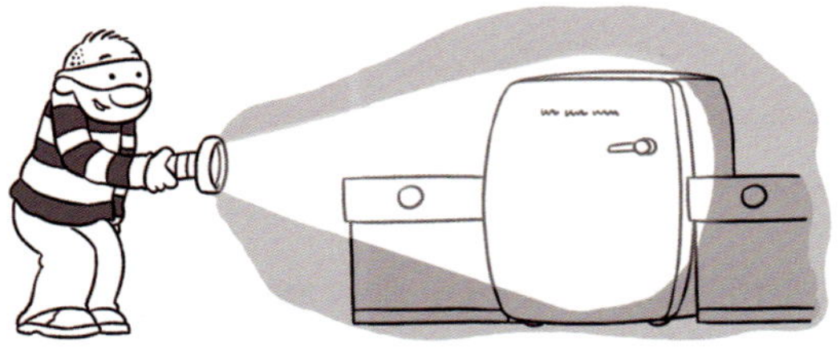

Singular	Plural
There's (is) a fridge in the kitchen.	There are two pictures.

1 Write *'s* or *are*.

1. There *'s* a lamp on the table.
2. There ______ clothes on the floor.
3. There ______ a bed in my room.
4. There ______ books on the desk.
5. There ______ a map near my desk.
6. There ______ a bag under the desk.
7. There ______ a TV in our living room.
8. There ______ six rooms in my house.
9. There ______ a dog in the kitchen.

2 Write sentences about your classroom.

1 board
There's a board in my classroom.
2 desks
3 door
4 teacher
5 poster

3 Write the correct words.

This is my bedroom. My bed's in front of the window. [1] *There* ______ some books near my bed. [2] ______ ______ a lamp on the table next to my bed. My radio is next to my lamp. On my desk [3] ______ ______ some pens and two cars. [4] ______ ______ three posters on the wall. My clothes aren't in the closet. They're on my chair and on the floor!

4 Write the sentences.

1 a sofa/the living room
There's a sofa in the living room.
2 a TV/the sofa
3 a table/the dining room
4 two pictures/the hall
5 a table/the kitchen
6 black cat/the stairs
7 a secret room/upstairs
8 a picture/the hall

– *There is/There are* – negative

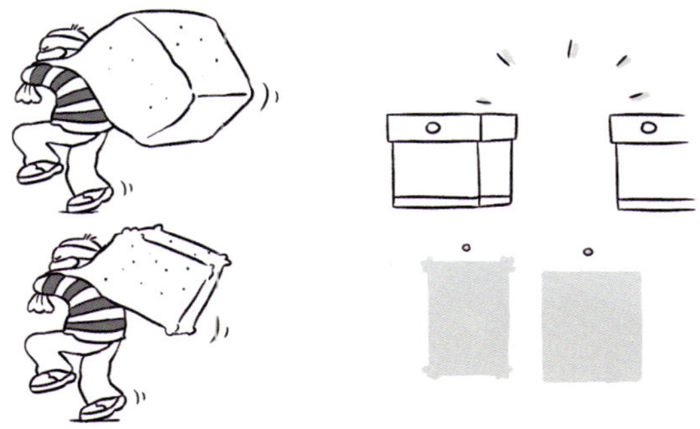

There isn't (is not) a fridge!
There aren't (are not) two pictures!

5 Make the sentences in exercise 1 negative.

1 *There isn't a lamp on the table.*

? *There is/There are* – questions and short answers

Singular

Is there a desk in your bedroom?	Yes, there is. No, there isn't.

Plural

Are there four chairs in the kitchen?	Yes, there are. No, there aren't.

6 Write the questions.

1 ______ two bathrooms in your house?
Are there two bathrooms in your house?
2 ______ a fridge in your kitchen?
3 ______ a piano in your kitchen?
4 ______ two sofas in your living room?
5 ______ a computer next to your bed?

7 In pairs, ask and answer the questions in exercise 6.

1 Are there two bathrooms in your house?
Yes, there are./No, there aren't.

8 Draw a plan of your room.

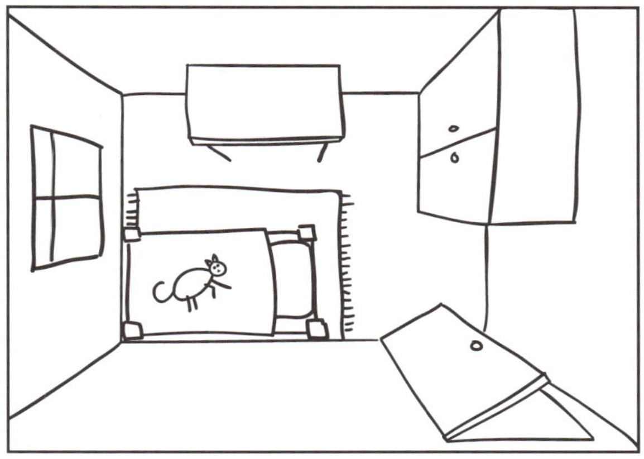

9 Write 6 sentences to describe your room.

There's a bed. There's a cat on the bed. Behind the bed is the window.

10 Ask your partner about his/her room.

- Are there two beds in your room?
- Is there a computer in your room?
- Where is it?

Extra

11 In pairs, A look at the picture of the house on page 19 for one minute and remember the details. Then close your book. B, ask A about the house.

B: *Is there a lamp in the house?*
A: *Yes, there is.*
B: *Where is it?*
A: *It's in the bedroom, next to the bed.*

2 Language

12 Listen and read.

Mark This is my mom's restaurant.
Joe Nice. "Jenny's" – your mom's name.
Mark I know, not very original, but…
Mom Hi guys! Welcome to Jenny's, Joe.
Joe Thanks.
Mom Can you please take Bonnie and Clyde home? I don't want them near the restaurant.
Mark I can't. I'm on my bike.
Joe Who are Bonnie and Clyde?
Mom Bonnie is Ellie's dog, and Clyde is Mark's dog.
Joe Cool!

Possessive 's – singular nouns

They're Ellie's puppies.

13 Write the correct answers.

1 Jenny is ______________ mom.
2 Jenny's is Ellie's ______________ restaurant.
3 ______________ bike is black.
4 Bonnie is ______________ dog.
5 Clyde is ______________ dog.
6 Joe is ______________ cousin.

14 Write sentences about the objects.

1. *This is Joe's backpack.*

2. ______________

3. ______________

4. ______________

5. ______________

Possessive 's – plural nouns

15 Match the pictures with the sentences.

1 The student's books.
2 The students' books.
3 The boy's dog.
4 The boys' dog.
5 The teachers' desk.
6 The teacher's desk.

A

B

C

D

E

F

2 Communicate

Vocabulary

1 Match the family words.

brother – sister

brother	mother
cousin	wife
father	grandmother
grandfather	sister
grandson	daughter
husband	granddaughter
nephew	aunt
son	cousin
uncle	niece

2 Listen and complete the names.

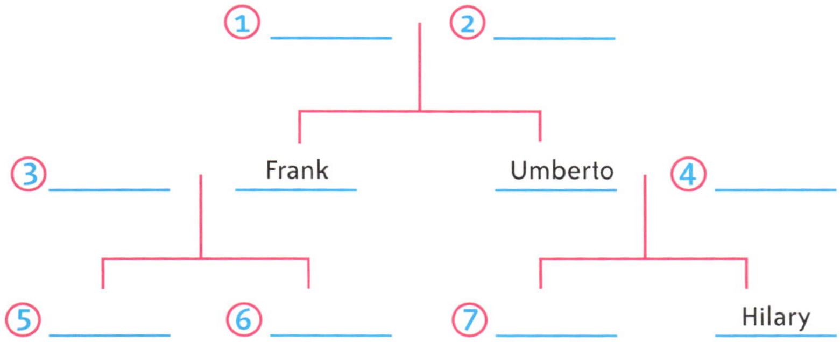

3 Ask and answer about the people in Ellie's family.

A: *Who's Rosaria?*
B: *She's Ellie's aunt.*

Talk about family

4 Joe is talking to Mark about his family. Listen and write the questions. Then repeat the dialog.

Joe Is ________ ________ grandfhather?
Mark Yes, it is.
Joe ________ 's his ________?
Mark George.
Joe Oh. ________ this your ________?
Mark No, it's my cousin. Her name is Hillary.
Joe ________ ________ is she?
Mark She's fourteen.
Joe Mmmm. She's cool!

5 Draw your family tree – don't write the names. Show your partner. Ask about your partner's family.

A: *Is that your brother?*
B: *Yes, it is.*
A: *How old is he?*
B: *He's…*
A: *What's his name?*
B: *Jim.*

Pronunciation

6 Can you hear the /h/ sound? Listen and circle the sound you hear. Then listen and repeat.

1 is/his
2 at/hat
3 I/Hi!
4 ow!/how
5 e/he

2 Skills

Barack Obama's Family

Barack Obama

This is Barack Obama, the 44th president of the United States of America and the first African American one. He is also a lawyer and a professor. Obama has a half-sister, the daughter of his mother and her Indonesian second husband, and six half-siblings from his Kenyan father's family.

Michelle Obama

This is his wife, Michelle Obama. She is the first African American First Lady. Michelle is really involved in social programs. She is a lawyer too. She has one brother.

Malia and Sasha Obama

These are their daughters Malia and Sasha. They study at Sidwell Friends School. They have a dog called Bo.

Marian Robinson

And this is Marian Robinson, Obama's mother-in-law. She lives in the White House too. She takes care of the girls when their parents are working.

Words you need

professor
siblings
parents

Reading

1 Read the text and check if the sentences are true (T) or false (F).

1. Barack's mother is Indonesian.
2. Marian is Michelle's mom.
3. Michelle is a professor and a lawyer.
4. Barack Obama has a big family.
5. Marian works at the White House.
6. Michelle and Barack are African.

Listening

2 Listen to the public opinion. Who is their favorite Obama?

1 ______________________________
2 ______________________________
3 ______________________________

3 Listen again. Write the missing names.

1 ________ is intelligent.
2 ________ only wears beautiful dresses!
3 ________ is a very good lawyer.
4 ________ is like a princess.
5 ________ is beautiful.
6 ________ needs to be the next president!

Speaking

4 In pairs, talk about your favorite family member.

A: *Who is your favorite family member?*
B: *My favorite family member is my cousin Julie.*
A: *What's she like?*
B: *She's very funny. She is a good friend.*

Writing

Punctuation (2)

- A capital letter begins a sentence.
- A full stop ends it.
  He's a sailor.
- A comma is common before "and" – it is used to indicate a division of ideas.
  He's from Greece, and his name's Philip.
- ? indicates a question.
  What's your name?

5 Correct these sentences. Use correct punctuation.

1 what's your name
2 my name's mark
3 i'm eleven and I'm a student
4 where are you from
5 i'm from England but my father is from Italy

Letter to a pen friend

6 Write to a pen friend about your home.

Research
Find a photo or draw a picture of your home.

Draft
Write a draft.

Hi Anna,
My house is in Westchester...
How many rooms are there?
There are...
How many people are there in your home?
Describe your favorite room in the house.
My favorite room is... , there's a...

Bye,
Lucy

Check
Check your draft – is the punctuation correct? Write the final version.

2 Look again

Language

1 Write affirmative (+) and negative (-) sentences.

1 TV/in the living room
+ *There is a TV in the living room.*
- *There isn't a TV in the living room.*
2 fridge/in kitchen
3 six oranges/in the fridge
4 two puppies/in the café
5 a piano/in the school

2 Write questions and short answers.

1 a pen/on your desk
Is there a pen on your desk? Yes, there is.
2 a desk/in your room
3 two beds/in your bedroom
4 pictures/on the walls/in your classroom
5 a computer/in your kitchen
6 clothes/on the floor/in your bedroom

3 Choose the correct answer.

1 This is a) Mark's b) Marks' bike.
2 There are two a) boy's b) boys' bags on the floor.
3 Patrick is a) Joe's b) Joes' dad.
4 Wow! Five a) actor's b) actors' Ferraris!

Vocabulary

4 Write the words.

Rooms
1 llah *hall*
2 borodem ______
3 lnviig omro ______
4 btarhoom ______
5 dniign omro ______
6 chenkti ______

Furniture
7 sfoa ______
8 fdgire ______
9 tbale ______
10 cpbuardo ______

5 Where are the keys? Write the correct preposition.

They're…

1 *in* the bag.
2 ______ the bag.
3 ______ the bag.
4 ______ the bag.

6 Write the correct

1 My father's brother is my *uncle*.
2 I'm a boy. I'm my aunt's ______.
3 My father's sister is my ______.
4 I'm a girl. I'm my aunt's ______.
5 My aunt's son is my ______.
6 My mother's dad is my ______.

Communication

7 Complete the dialog.

A: Is that your brother?
B: No, he's my cousin.
A: [1] ______________?
B: He's thirteen.
A: [2] ______________?
B: He's from Miami – in Florida.
A: [3] ______________?
B: Eddie.

Now you can…

	☹ 😐 ☺
use the verb *to be* in the singular – affirmative/negative (*ex 1*) – questions/answers (*ex 2*)	
use possessive nouns (*ex 3*)	
name rooms/furniture (*ex 4*)	
use prepositions (*ex 5*)	
name family members (*ex 6*)	
write personal questions (*ex 7*)	

Culture spot

Typical age children leave home in different countries

When do children "leave the nest" in different countries?

Typically, Americans want to leave their parents' home when they go to university, around the age of eighteen or nineteen. They want to be independent and work. Children in other countries (for example, Brazil and Spain) are very different. They want to save money, so they "leave the nest" after they finish university, or sometimes only after they find a husband or wife.

1 **To "leave the nest" is to**
a. go to university.
b. move out of your parents' house.
c. have children.

2 **Sons and daughters want to leave their parents' home when they are teenagers in**
a. the USA. b. Spain. c. Brazil.

3 **American teenagers want to**
a. be independent. b. save money. c. find a husband or wife.

3 He has a beard

Presentation

1 Listen and read.

Miss Brown	OK! Do you have your costumes?
Ellie	Yes, we're ready! Who are you, May?
May	I'm Robin Hood. Look, I have long, black hair and a green hat.
Ellie	It's a nice hat, but Robin Hood has a beard and he doesn't have glasses.
Mark	And he's a man!
Miss Brown	You're a very good Robin Hood, May.
Ellie	And I'm Maid Marian!
Mark	No way Ellie! Maid Marian has straight, blond hair.
Ellie	Well I'm Maid Marian with *curly*, blond hair. OK?
Joe	Hey, Mark! Look at this horrible character! He has a really ugly face!
Mark	Where?
Joe	Here! It's a monster!
Mark	Really? My reflection in the mirror? Very funny, Joe.

Expressions

- We're ready!
- No way
- Very funny!
- Really?

Comprehension

2 True or false?

1 They are ready.
2 In the play, Ellie is Robin Hood.
3 May has a green hat.
4 May has a beard.
5 Ellie has straight, blond hair.
6 There is a mirror in front of Mark.

Vocabulary

3 Match the words with the pictures. Listen, check and repeat the words.

arm
beard
ears
eyes
face (M)
foot
fur
hand
head (F)
leg
mustache
mouth
nose
scar
tail
tooth

Grammar bite

Irregular plurals

foot → feet
tooth → teeth

4 Match the sentences to these characters. Then write a sentence about you.

1 He has curly, red hair.
2 She has long, straight hair.
3 He has short, blond hair.
4 He doesn't have hair – he's bald!
5 I have ______________ , ______________ hair.

5 Listen to the descriptions. Who are they?

1 ____________ 2 __________ 3 __________ 4 __________

Pronunciation

6 /ð/ or /θ/. Listen and choose the sound you hear. Then listen and repeat.

bathroom brother month mother mouth
the there this tooth with three

3 Language

1 Read the newspaper story. How many hackers are there? ________

POLICE SEARCH FOR FACEBOOK HACKERS

There is an international police search for four computer hackers. Social media websites like Facebook and Twitter are their specialty.

Here are their descriptions – Paul Blane has short, black hair, a mustache and a beard, a gold tooth and brown eyes. Amelia Spink has curly blond hair, green eyes and glasses. Tania Johnson has long red hair and a scar on her face. Dave Bruce is bald. He has blue eyes and a scar on his nose. Call 1-800-555-COPS if you have any information.

2 Read the newspaper story again. Write the correct names for each hacker.

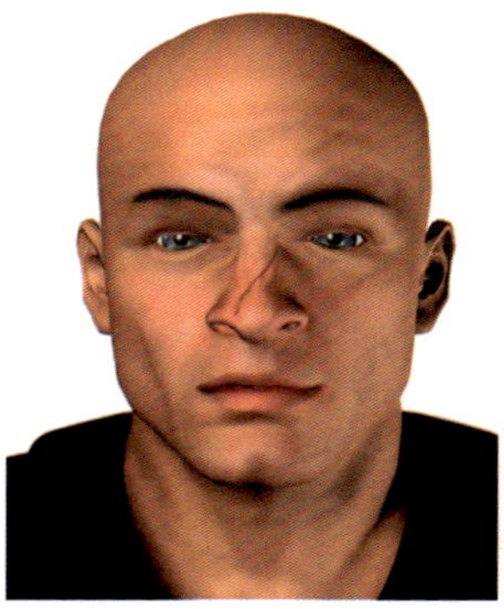

A ______________

B ______________

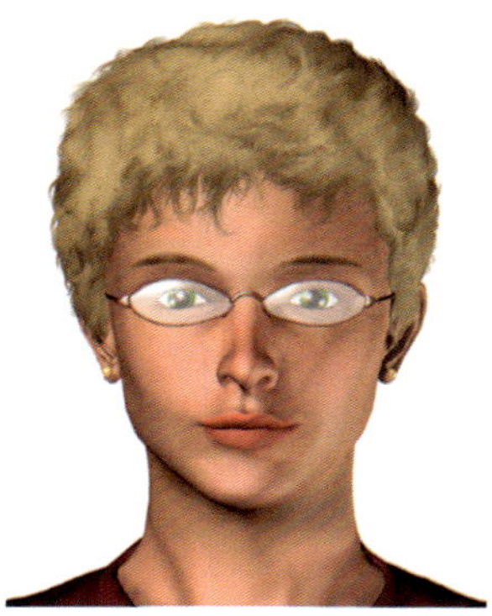

C ______________

D ______________

+ *Has* – affirmative

Singular		Plural
I	have	We have
You	have	You have
He	has	They have
She	has	
It	has	

3 Write *have* or *has*.

1 Amelia ___*has*___ glasses.
2 Dave __________ a scar on his nose.
3 Tania __________ long, red hair.
4 She __________ a scar on her face.
5 You __________ curly hair too.
6 We __________ green eyes.
7 I __________ a gold tooth.
8 My aunt __________ a white car.

4 Mark the sentences that are not possible.

Example:
I have brown eyes.
I have green feet. _*x*_

1 I have blond hair. ___
2 I have a scar on my teeth. ___
3 My dog has glasses. ___
4 My cousin has a tail. ___
5 My dad has a beard. ___
6 I have long, blue eyes. ___

Has – negative

Singular		Contractions
I do		I don't
You do		You don't
We do	not have	We don't
They do		They don't
He/She/It does		He/She/It doesn't

Adjective order – double adjectives

Paul Blane has short black hair.
Amelia Spink has curly blond hair.
Tania Johnson has long red hair.

5 Make these sentences negative.

1 Marie has short hair.
Marie does not/doesn't have short hair.
2 Pete has a big nose.
3 Erik has a pen.
4 She has green eyes.
5 Mark and Ellie have a key.
6 Madonna has short hair.
7 Shrek has blue eyes.
8 My sister has a beard!

6 Look at the newspaper again. Write true sentences about the hackers and about you.

1 Paul Blane/short hair
Paul Blane has short hair.
2 Tania Johnson/a mustache
3 Tania/a scar on her face
4 Dave Bruce/green eyes
5 Amelia/glasses
6 Paul Blane/red hair
7 your teacher/a beard
8 I/a gold tooth

7 Write the sentences in the correct order.

1 hair/has/brown/Mark/short
Mark has short brown hair.
2 Ariana/blond/long/has/hair
3 red/dad/beard/my/short/has/a
4 teacher/little/our/mustache/black/a/has
5 beautiful/cat/your/has/fur/white
6 have/eyes/green/big/you

8 Read the descriptions and write the name of a classmate.

1 She has long black hair.
____
2 He has short brown hair.
____
3 They have big brown eyes.
____
4 She has perfect white teeth.
____
5 He doesn't have short black hair.
____
6 They don't have curly blond hair.
____

Extra

9 Write four sentences about you. Talk about your hair, your eye color, glasses and your beard!

I have long brown hair and brown eyes.

3 Language

Has – questions and short answers

Singular	Contractions
Do we have long hair?	Yes, we do. No, we don't.
Does he have long hair?	Yes, he does. No, he doesn't.

Ugly Betty

Obi Wan Kenobi

The Nutty Professor

10 **Look at the photos. Write questions about the people.**

1 Obi/short hair?
Does Obi have short hair?
2 the Professor/long hair
3 Ugly Betty/glasses?
4 the Professor and Obi/black hair?
5 they/big mustaches?
6 Obi/glasses?
7 Ugly Betty/beard?
8 you/beard?

11 **In pairs, ask and answer the questions in exercise 10.**

A: *Does Obi have short hair?*
B: *No, he doesn't.*

12 **Listen. Which is the correct picture?**

1

2

3

4

13 **In pairs, A choose a person from this page. B, ask questions to find the person.**

B: *Does he/she have long hair?*
A: *Yes, he does.*

14 **Draw a picture of this person.**

Auguste Lemonde is old – he's seventy-two. He has gray hair and glasses. He has a black beard and a mustache. He has a scar on his nose. He has big green eyes.

3 Communicate

Vocabulary

1 Match the words to the pictures. Listen, check and repeat the words.

beautiful
smart
confident
fat
friendly (A)
horrible
nice
old
short
shy
strong
tall
thin
ugly
weak
young

2 Write the opposites.

1 tall	2 strong	3 horrible
4 young	5 ugly	6 thin

Learning Tip

Remembering vocabulary

Write words with their opposites. You can remember them this way.

Describe people

3 Choose a person from your class. Draw a 'wanted' poster. Don't show your partner!

4 Who is it? In pairs, ask and answer. Then show your poster.

- boy/girl
- tall/thin/strong
- hair/eyes/glasses/a scar
- name?

A: *Is it a boy or a girl?*
B: *A boy.*

3 Skills

A MOVIE REVIEW

Puss in Boots is a confident character. He's very small, but he's brave and he's a good friend. He has ginger fur and beautiful eyes.

The donkey doesn't really have a name. In the movie, his name is Donkey. He has long ears and big teeth. He's fat, has short legs, and is very funny.

MY FAVORITE MOVIE

Shrek 2 **is my favorite movie. It's a love story but it's funny too. It's a great movie!**

Princess Fiona is tall and thin and she's very strong. She has big blue eyes and long red hair. Sometimes she's horrible.

Shrek is a monster. He has a big head and green ears. He's bald and has a big nose and mouth. He's big and ugly, and he's not very friendly. His wife is Princess Fiona.

Reading

Words you need

brave
ginger
funny
monster
friendly

1 Read and answer the questions.

1 Which character is confident?
2 Which character doesn't have a real name?
3 Which character has big teeth?
4 Who is sometimes horrible?
5 Who is Shrek's wife?

Listening

2 Listen and match the descriptions with the characters. Write the number next to the name.

Prince Charming ___

King Harold ___

The Dragon ___

The Queen ___

3 Listen again and write the correct word.

King Harold is [1] _____ and [2] _____.
He has [3] _____ hair and brown [4] _____.
He's Princess Fiona's [5] _____. He isn't very [6] _____.
Prince Charming is [7] _____ but he isn't [8] _____. He has [9] _____ hair and [10] _____ eyes. He has a horrible [11] _____ and he's [12] _____ too.

Speaking

4 In pairs, A talk about your favorite movie character. Don't say who it is. B guess the character.

A: *He's friendly/brave/horrible/ugly…*
He has a cowboy hat/a long nose…
B: *Does he have…?*
Is it Woody from Toy Story?

Writing

Not repeating the subject

Don't repeat the subject again and again in one sentence. Your writing will be more natural:

Unnecessary repetition:
He is fat, he has short legs, and he is very funny.

Better:
He's fat, has short legs, and is very funny.

5 Delete unnecessary words in these sentences.

1. That movie is excellent. It is funny and it has good characters.
2. The teacher is very good. He has fun classes and he isn't boring.
3. We are lucky. We have a good house, we have food, and we have education.

A movie review

6 Write a review about your favorite movie.

Research
Think about a movie you like. Find pictures or photos of the characters.

Draft
Write a draft.

What's your favorite movie? Why?
It's great/funny
It's a love/adventure story
Who are the actors?
Which actors are good/great/bad?
Describe two characters

Check
Check your draft – do you repeat the subject? Write the final version.

3 Look again

Language

1 Write *have* or *has*.

1 He *has* curly hair.
2 She ______ blue eyes.
3 I ______ black hair.
4 You ______ blue eyes.
5 They ______ blond hair.
6 I ______ a scar.

2 Write the questions.

1 *Does she have* ______ blond hair? (she)
2 ______ green eyes? (he)
3 ______ long hair? (they)
4 ______ a mustache? (he)
5 ______ nice teeth? (I)
6 ______ a scar? (you)

3 Write the adjectives in the sentences.

big black blue ginger green
horrible nice perfect thin white

1 Puss in Boots has *nice ginger* fur.
2 She has ______ eyes.
3 I have ______ teeth.
4 Shrek has ______ ears.
5 My dad has a ______ mustache.

Vocabulary

4 Write the words.

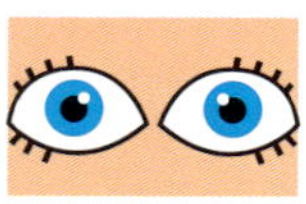
1 *eyes*

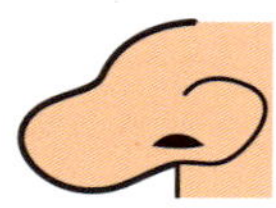
2 ______

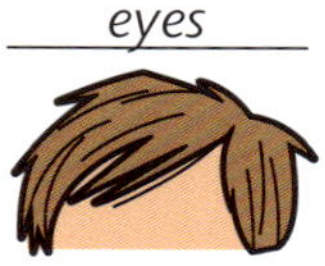
3 ______

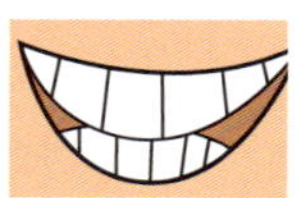
4 ______

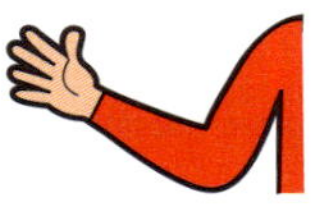
5 ______

6 ______

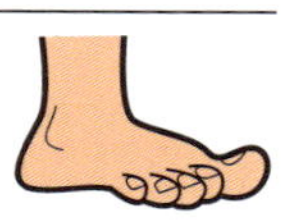
7 ______

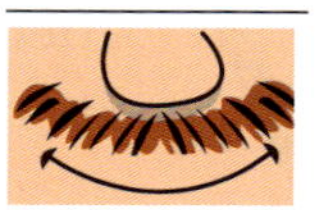
8 ______

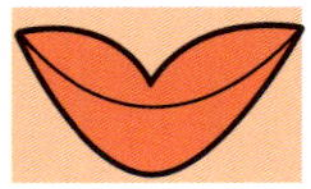
9 ______

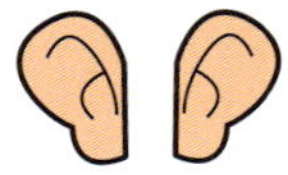
10 ______

5 Complete the words.

1 b e *a* *u* t *i* f *u* l
2 s ___ ___ r t
3 c ___ n f ___ d ___ n t
4 f r ___ ___ n d l ___
5 h ___ r r ___ b l ___
6 s t r ___ n g
7 t ___ l l

Communication

6 Complete the dialog.

short shy hair mustache

A: Does your dad have long [1] *hair* ?
B: No, he doesn't. It's [2] ______ and curly.
A: Does he have a [3] ______ ?
B: Yes, he does – and a beard.
A: Is he friendly?
B: Yes, he is but he is very [4] ______ .

7 Write a dialog about a friend. Use exercise 6 to help you.

Now you can…	☹ 😐 ☺
use *have* – affirmative (*ex 1*) – questions (*ex 2*)	
use two adjectives in the correct order to – talk about body parts (*ex 3*) – name body parts (*ex 4*) – write adjectives (*ex 5*) – describe people (*ex 6 and 7*)	

Game

Follow these instructions:

- Use a die to move.
- In each square, follow the instruction or answer the question. If you are not correct, you go back one square.

4 She takes piano lessons with me

Presentation

1 **Listen and read.**

Expressions
- He looks…
- I see…

Mom Who is that?
Mark That's James. He sits next to me in English class.
Mom Who is this guy here? He looks nice.
Mark Kurt? Yeah, he is nice. We play basketball together sometimes. But he doesn't play very well.
Mom And what about that boy?
Mark Oh, that's Ellie's boyfriend.
Mom Does Ellie have a boyfriend? What's his name?
Mark Nick. He takes the bus with me every morning.
Mom I see. And what about this cute girl?
Mark Who – Natalie?
Mom Yeah. Does she go to your school?
Mark Yes, she does. She takes piano lessons with me on Thursdays. She's really nice. She knows judo! And she speaks fluent French! And she –
Mom Hmm… Do you smell that?
Mark Smell what?
Mom The smell of romance in the air!
Mark Mom!!!

Comprehension

2 Read and answer the questions.

1 What class do Mark and James have together?
2 Is Kurt a good basketball player?
3 Who is Nick?
4 What do Mark and Nick do together?
5 What musical instrument does Mark play?

Vocabulary

3 Which activities can you see in the pictures? Listen, check and repeat the words.

do my homework
get dressed
get up (A)
go to bed
go to school
take a shower
take the bus
take piano lessons
have breakfast
have dinner
have lunch
play video games
play soccer

Learning Tip
Storing vocabulary
Store words together that use the same verb.
get up
get dressed

Learning Tip

4 Listen to Mark's day. What does he do?

1 *get up* 2 ______ 3 ______ 4 ______ 5 ______

5 In pairs, cover the activities in exercise 3. Then ask and answer about them.

A: *What's A?*
B: *Get up.*

4 Language

+ Simple present – affirmative

I/You	work.
He/She/It	works.
We/You/They	work.

– Simple present – negative

I/You	don't	
He/She/It	doesn't	work.
We/You/They	don't	

don't = do not
doesn't = does not

Grammar bite

he, she, it

- For *he, she, it* add *s* → *walks*
- Verbs ending in a vowel *-s/-sh/-ch* add *-es*, → *goes/passes/washes/watches*
- Verbs ending in *y* change to *ies* study → *studies*

1 Write the correct form of the verbs.

A day in the life of my dad

My dad's name is Jimu Ruan. He (get up) [1] gets up at 6:30. He (have) [2] ______ breakfast with my mom then he (go) [3] _____ to work. He (ride) [4] _______ his bike to work. He (visit) [5] _______ a lot of people. He's a doctor. At four I (do) [6] _____ my homework. My dad comes home late and he (use) [7] _____ his computer then he reads the newspaper. At nine o'clock we (watch) [8] _____ TV. Well, I (watch) [9] _______TV and he (go) [10] _______ to sleep!

By May

2 Circle *don't* or *doesn't*.

A day in the life of my mom

My mom's name is Shuo. She [1] don't/doesn't get up at 6:30. She gets up at six! She [2] don't/doesn't have breakfast with me – she has breakfast with my dad. I [3] don't/doesn't see my dad in the morning. My mom [4] don't/doesn't go to work – she is at home with my brother, Liang. He [5] don't/doesn't go to school – he's only two. My dad [6] don't/doesn't have dinner with us. He comes home late but he [7] don't/doesn't work on the weekend. We [8] don't/doesn't get up early at the weekend. ☺

By May

Simple present – questions

Do	I/you	
Does	he/she/it	work?
Do	we/you/they	

Simple present – questions and short answers

Do you know? Yes, I do./No, I don't.
Does he know? Yes, he does./No, he doesn't.

Yes,/No,	I/you	do/don't.
Yes,/No,	he/she/it	does/doesn't.
Yes,/No,	we/you/they	do/don't.

3 Write the correct form of *do* and the verb.

1 *Does* May's dad (work) *work* at home?
2 ____ you (walk) ____ to school?
3 ____ Jimu (visit) ____ a lot of people?
4 ____ May (talk) ____ to her dad?
5 ____ May and Liang (walk) ____ to school?
6 ____ Shuo and May (have) ____ dinner with Jimu?
7 ____ Liang (go) ____ to school?
8 ____ they (have) ____ breakfast at six?
9 ____ you (walk) ____ to school with Liang?
10 ____ your dad (work) ____ here?

4 Make questions from the sentences.

1 Jimu gets up at six.
Does Jimu get up at six?
2 He rides his bike to work.
3 He visits a lot of people.
4 He uses a computer at home.
5 May has breakfast with her parents.
6 Liang goes to school.
7 They get up early at the weekend.
8 Jimu comes home late.

5 Answer the questions in exercise 4 with short answers.

A: *Does Jimu get up at six?*
B: *No, he doesn't.*

Extra

6 In pairs, ask and answer about your friends and family.

- ride a bike to work
- play the guitar
- speak French
- have a shower every morning
- walk to school
- do homework every day
- work at home
- you decide

A: *Does your dad ride a bike to work?*
B: *Yes, he does.*

4 Language

7 **Complete the text with the correct form of the verb.**

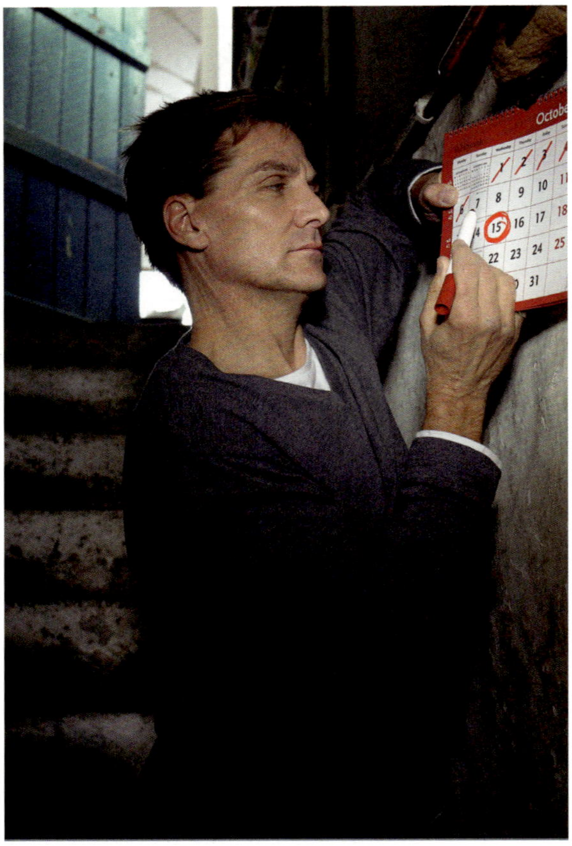

Mr. Murray's Routine

At seven thirty, Mr. Murray (have) [1] *has* breakfast with his wife Roberta and his son Joe. He (read) [2] _______ the newspaper. At ten o'clock, he (run) [3] _______ on his treadmill. At one o'clock he (go) [4] _______ to his home office, he (talk) [5] _______ on the phone, he (work) [6] _______ on his computer and he (write) [7] _______ letters. There's a calendar on the wall. He looks at it and counts the days. At four, his son (come) [9] _______ home. Mr. Murray (help) [10] _______ him with his homework. At seven they (watch) [11] _______ TV or (play) [12] _______ a game. He doesn't go out.

8 **Write questions about Mr. Murray.**

1 have breakfast with Joe?
Does he have breakfast with Joe?
2 go running in the street?
3 use his computer?
4 write letters?
5 look at the calendar?
6 go out?

9 **In pairs, ask and answer the questions.**

A: *Does he have breakfast with Joe?*
B: *Yes, he does./No, he doesn't.*

Pronunciation

10 **/s/, /z/ or /iz/. Listen and choose the sound you hear. Then listen and repeat.**

eat**s** */s/* go**es** us**es** choos**es**
take**s** do**es** meet**s** come**s**
run**s** walk**s** watch**es**

Object pronouns

Singular		Plural	
I	me	we	us
you	you	you	you
he	him	they	them
she	her		
it	it		

11 **Write the correct object pronoun.**

1 He doesn't talk to (the men) *them* .
2 I can't find (my shoes) ________ .
3 Please phone (Ana) ________ .
4 Mom swims with (me and my sister) ________ .
5 Can you hear (the sound) ________ ?
6 I help (my dad) ________ on Monday.
7 Can you see (me and my friend) ________ on the street?

4 Communicate

Vocabulary

1 **Match the times to the clocks. Listen, check and repeat the times.**

It's one o'clock.
It's eleven o'clock.

It's one thirty.
It's eleven thirty.

It's six fifteen.
It's five forty-five. (A)

It's midnight.
It's 3 A.M.
It's 3 P.M.

2 **Point at the times above. Then ask and answer in pairs.**

A: *What time is it?*
B: *It's one o'clock.*

3 **Complete the diary. Listen, check and repeat the days.**

FEBRUARY	
Mo ____________	**Weekend**
Tu ____________	**Sa** ____________
We ____________	**Su** ____________
Th ____________	***Notes***
Fr ____________	

Saturday
Wednesday
Monday
Thursday
Sunday
Friday
Tuesday

Talk about routine

4 **Listen and complete the dialog. Then practice it in pairs.**

Teacher What time do you *get* ________ on Mondays?
Student Um, I get up at ________________ .
Teacher Oh. And what time do you ________ to ________ ?
Student I go to bed at ____________ .
Teacher ____________ ! On Mondays?

5 **In pairs, A write the times you do these activities in a school day. B, interview your partner.**

- get up
- have dinner
- go home
- do your homework

A: *What time do you get up?*
B: *At six forty-five.*

Grammar bite

at **or** ***on*****?**

On Monday
On the weekend
At nine

4 Skills

www.mebo.com

mebo Join the fun and make new friends

Friends | Photos | Blog | Video | Search | quick | advanced

Login
Register
Help

Win!
Games

Me home
Advice

Sport
Fun zone

SINDY

Sindy's Blog. August 24th

Hi everybody! I'm at Forest Camp and it's great! There are sixty kids here and we all sleep in little cabins. I'm in Acorn Cabin with five other girls.

Mrs. Jackson wakes us up at six o'clock. SIX!!! I get up and take a shower. Then we have breakfast – bacon and eggs, cereal and fruit. After that, we clean our cabins and Mrs. Jackson checks them. First, we play volleyball, soccer or tennis… then we learn a new activity. I can ride a horse now! We have lunch at one, in the camp café or we have a picnic. After lunch we have a rest and play cards, chess or read. Then we go to the beach and swim. Dinner is at six. In the evening we have a campfire. We sing songs and tell scary stories… whoooooo! It's cool! I have new friends and I don't want to go back to school!

Reading

1 Is this text from a book, a website or a magazine?

2 Read about Sindy and answer the questions.

1 Where is Sindy?
2 Does she like it?
3 What time does she get up?
4 What new thing can Sindy do now?
5 What do they do after lunch?
6 What do they do at the campfire?

Words you need

cabins
picnic
play cards
have a campfire

Listening

3 Listen to the students. What do they do in the evening?

4 Listen again and write the times.

Rachel

get up ______
go to school/work ______
go home ______
go to bed ______

Jamie

get up ______
go to school/work ______
go home ______
go to bed ______

Tania

get up ______
go to school/work ______
go home ______
go to bed ______

Speaking

5 In pairs talk about a person you know. Answer the questions.

- Who/it?
- What time/get up?
- What time/go to school/work?
- What/do in evening?

Writing

Linking sentences (3) – *first/then/after that*

First, we do activities. Then we have lunch After that we go to the beach.

6 Write sentences. Connect them using *first*, *then* and *after that*.

1. I get up/get dressed/have breakfast
   First I get up, then I get dressed and after that I have breakfast.
2. she/go home/watch TV/go to bed
3. they/get up/have breakfast/go to work
4. I get up/have a shower/go to school
5. we have dinner/play soccer/go to bed
6. he does his exercises/take a shower/go to work

My webpage

7 Make a webpage. Write about a day in your life.

Research
Make notes about your daily routine. Find or draw pictures to add to your writing.

Draft
Write a draft.

Introduce yourself
This is a day in the life of...
Describe your morning routine
I get up at... . Then... , after that...
Describe your routine in the day
At three o'clock I...
Describe your evening routine
At nine o'clock I watch TV. Then...

Check
Check your draft – are the linking words correct? Write the final version.

4 Look again

Language

1 Write the correct form of the verb.

1 I (have) _have_ an omelet for breakfast.
2 Paula (use) ______ her cell phone at school.
3 Mr. Palmer (play) ______ the electric guitar.
4 Sam (take) ______ the bus every day.
5 You (run) ______ fast!
6 Those guys (play) ______ video games every day!

2 Rewrite these sentences as negatives.

1 You go to Moorside School.
You don't go to Moorside School.
2 Mr. Anderson speaks Russian.
3 My teacher gives us a lot of homework.
4 I have breakfast with my family.
5 Bella plays the piano.

3 Write the sentences as questions.

1 do your homework on the bus? (you)
Do you do your homework on the bus?
2 play basketball? (she)
3 get up at 6 A.M? (your family)
4 use a computer? (your mom)

4 Complete the short answers for exercise 3.

1 Yes, I __________ .
2 No, she __________ .
3 No, they __________ .
4 Yes, she __________ .

Vocabulary

5 Complete with the correct verb.

1 _get_ up
2 ______ a shower
3 ______ breakfast
4 ______ dressed
5 ______ my homework
6 ______ soccer
7 ______ guitar lessons
8 ______ the train

6 Complete the times.

1 It's one _o'clock_.
2 It's two ________.
3 It's two ________ .
4 It's ten ________.
5 It's three ________ .
6 It's five ________.

Communication

7 Complete the dialog.

You ______________________________ ?
Tony I get up at eight o'clock.
You ______________________________ ?
Tony I go to school at eight thirty.
You ______________________________ ?
Tony I go home at three thirty.
You ______________________________ ?
Tony I go to bed at ten o'clock.

Now you can...	☹ 😐 ☺
use simple present – affirmative (*ex 1*) – negative (*ex 2*) – questions (*ex 3*) – short answers (*ex 4*)	
use routine verbs (*ex 5*)	
tell the time (*ex 6*)	
ask routine questions (*ex 7*)	

Culture spot

School in China is not easy

At the age of 12, Zhuzhu has toys, beautiful clothes, and even a piano. But Zhuzhu doesn't have time to play. She goes to bed late, with a mountain of homework to do. Like other Chinese children her age, Zhuzhu goes to school from Monday to Friday, nine hours a day. On the weekend, she gets up early for piano lessons on Saturday and Sunday morning, then private math and English classes in the afternoon.

Students study at a middle school classroom in a village in Jinzhai County, east China's Anhui Province.

China's children study at school between 8 to 12 hours every day, get up early and go to bed late. They don't have play time, or they only have a little play time. In fact, only 40% of Chinese children have friends to play with.

An Hui, Zhuzhu's mom, knows that her daughter doesn't have sleep or playtime, "We have no other choice," she said. "This is the reality of China".

Source: http://www.chinadaily.com.cn/china/2007-05/13/content_871182.htm

1 Read the text.

1 What musical instrument does Zhuzhu play?
2 How many days per week does Zhuzhu go to school?
3 When does she take piano lessons?
4 What does she study on Sunday afternoon?

2 Same or different?

1 Do you study at school more than eight hours per day?
2 Do you go to bed late? Why (not)?

5 What are you watching?

Presentation

1 Listen and read.

Expressions
- You're kidding!
- cheer for
- of course
- anyway

Ellie	What are you watching, Mark?
Mark	I'm watching a soccer game.
Ellie	Who's playing?
Mark	The USA are playing against Brazil.
Ellie	Cool! What's the score?
Mark	Brazil is winning, of course. Five to one.
Ellie	Five to one? You're kidding! That's horrible.
Mark	No it's not. I'm cheering for Brazil!
Ellie	Why?
Mark	The Brazilian team has talent.
Ellie	No, Brazil has Neymar! Anyway, Americans have talent too! See?
Mark	What are you doing?
Ellie	I'm dribbling the ball, like a soccer player.
Mark	You're dancing like you have two left feet.
Ellie	What?
Mark	I'm just kidding!

Comprehension

2 Write True (T) or False (F) for each sentence.

1 Mark is watching television.
2 Ellie is cheering for the American team.
3 Mark doesn't like Brazil.
4 Neymar is a soccer player.
5 Ellie is dancing.

Vocabulary

3 Match the words with the pictures. Listen, check and repeat the words.

doctor
soccer player
farmer
firefighter
journalist
mechanic (A)
nurse
police officer
receptionist
lawyer
soldier
student
teacher

Learning Tip
Marking stress
Mark the stress on new words.
dóctor

4 What's the job? In pairs, A think of a job but don't say what it is. B ask questions.

- What time does he/she start work?
- Does he/she work inside or outside?
- Does he/she wear a uniform? What is it?

B: *Is she a farmer?*
A: *Yes, she is. / No, she isn't.*

Pronunciation

5 /ə/ Listen and repeat.

1 doct**or** 2 farm**er** 3 soldi**er**
4 teach**er** 5 work**er** 6 act**or**

5 Language

Hi, Grandma! Yes, we're all having a good time! Aunt Pat is dancing with Uncle Paul – he's wearing a Dracula costume, and she's a policewoman. Louisa is fighting with Tommy in the kitchen – she's wearing a doctor's uniform, and he's a soldier. Mom's bringing my birthday cake! Bye!

+ Present continuous – affirmative

I	'm	reading.
You	're	
He/She/It	's	
We/You/They	're	

– Present continuous – negative

I	'm not	reading.
You	aren't	
He/She/It	isn't	
We/You/They	aren't	

1 Complete the gaps with the correct form of the verb.

I (talk) [1] *am talking* to my grandmother on the phone. I (tell) [2] ______ her about my birthday party. My uncle (dance) [3] ________ with my aunt. My brother Tommy is in the kitchen with my sister. They (fight) [4] ______. We (wear) [5] ______ costumes. My uncle (wear) [6] _______ a Dracula costume and my sister (wear) [7] _________ a doctor's uniform. It's time to go – my mom (bring) [8] __________ my cake into the room.

2 Rewrite these sentences as negatives.

1 I'm talking to my grandfather.
I'm not talking to my grandfather.
2 My uncle's dancing with my sister.
3 My brother and sister are talking.
4 We're wearing school uniform.
5 My sister's wearing a soldier's uniform.
6 My mom is bringing my present.

Present continuous – questions

Am	I	reading?
Are	you	
Is	he/she/it	
Are	we/you/they	

3 Make questions from the sentences.

1 We're having a good time.
Are we having a good time?
2 Aunt Pat is dancing.
3 Uncle Paul is wearing a Dracula costume.
4 Louisa and Tommy are fighting.
5 Mom's bringing my cake.

4 Write questions about the people in exercise 1.

1 his mom/laughing?
Is his mom laughing?
2 his sister/sitting down?
3 his brother/eating?
4 his uncle and aunt/dancing?
5 they/having a good time?

Present continuous – short answers

5 Answer these questions with a positive and a negative short answer. Then circle the true answer.

1 Are you writing with a pencil?
Yes, I am. No, I'm not.
2 Is your teacher standing up?
3 Is your teacher wearing a hoodie?
4 Are your friends working?
5 Are you using your cell phone?
6 Are you thinking about food?

Present continuous – *Wh-* Questions

What	am	I	reading?
Why	are	you	
How	is	he/she/it	
Where	are	we/you/they	

6 Make *wh-* questions from the words.

1 why/you/read this book?
Why are you reading this book?
2 what/your teacher/do?
3 where/your friends/go today?
4 who/your teacher/look at?
5 what/she wear now?

5 Language

7 In the text, find examples of…

1 the present continuous affirmative.
2 the present continuous negative.
3 the present continuous question.

8 Correct the sentences.

1 Ellie is studying for a test.
No, she's not. She's going to the (Maroon 5) concert.
2 Ellie is standing in her living room.
3 Joe is speaking with Ellie.
4 Ellie is going to the library.
5 Joe is reading.
6 Joe is waiting for Ellie.

9 Connect the words that go together.

1 read	___ a test
2 brush	___ your teeth
3 watch	___ music
4 play	___ a book
5 study for	___ soccer
6 listen to	___ TV

10 Write what they are doing in the pictures.

1 *She's brushing her teeth.*

2 ______________________

3 ______________________

4 ______________________

5 ______________________

6 ______________________

5 Communicate

Vocabulary

1 Match the words with the pictures. Listen, check and repeat the words.

- dive
- gymnastics
- karate
- fish
- hang out with friends
- lie on the beach
- basketball (A)
- soccer
- ping pong
- tennis
- volleyball
- shop
- skateboard
- ski
- sunbathe
- surf
- swim

2 In pairs, mime an activity and guess what is happening.

A: *What am I doing?*
B: *Are you skiing?*

Chat on the phone

3 Listen and complete the phone conversation.

Ellie	Hi Joe, it's Ellie.
Joe	Hey! Ellie! How [1] *are you* ?
Ellie	Great thanks. Are you [2] ______ a good vacation?
Joe	It's brilliant!
Ellie	What [3] ______ you [4] ______ ?
Joe	Oh, you know. I'm [5] ______ soccer and lying on the beach.
Ellie	What? Right now?
Joe	No! I'm eating an ice cream and I'm [6] ______ to you!
Ellie	Oops! I can't talk now! I'm [7] ______ my mom's [8] ______ ! See you [9] ______ Joe!
Joe	Bye, Ellie. [10] ______ for calling.

4 In pairs, practice saying the phone conversation.

5 You are on vacation. Chat with a friend on the phone about what you are doing right now. Use the phone phrases.

- It's…
- Hi/Hello/Hey!
- How are you?
- Thanks for calling.
- I can't talk now.
- Bye!
- See you later!

5 Skills

Mom's watching for sharks

Linda, Grant, and their children Susie (8) and Patrick (13) are sailing around the world on their boat *Seabreeze*. Patrick writes an Internet diary for his homework.

Today we're near the equator, in the middle of the Pacific Ocean. Our next stop is New Zealand. It's so hot we're swimming, diving and sunbathing — but right now I'm writing in my diary, obviously.

What are we all doing? Well, right now Dad's diving under the boat because he's cleaning it. (He's an engineer so he loves cleaning things!) Right now, Mom's watching for sharks. She sometimes hits the boat and shouts "Shark!" We all jump out of the water. Susie isn't swimming right now. She's making tuna sandwiches for lunch again. She's always hungry!

Here are some photos. In the first one, Susie is dressed as a pirate for our party because we're crossing the equator. In the other photo is Polly – my parrot. She is brushing her teeth! I love sailing the boat, but it's hard work! I do three hours of schoolwork every day. (This diary is my writing homework. Mom always checks my *speling*, ha ha.) I often chat to my friends on the radio but I miss them.

Reading

Words you need

in the middle of
next stop
sharks
tuna sandwiches

1 **Look at the title and the pictures and guess what the text is about.**

2 **Read the diary and answer the questions.**

1 Who's writing the diary?
2 Where is the boat right now?
3 What's Patrick's dad doing right now?
4 What's his mom doing?
5 What does Patrick do every day?
6 How much schoolwork does he do?

Listening

3 Patrick's talking on the boat's radio. Listen and answer the questions.

1 Who is he talking to?
2 Where is the boat?
3 Where is Patrick?

4 Listen again. What are they doing right now?

Dad… Patrick…
Mom… Polly…
Susie…

Speaking

5 In pairs, talk on the radio. A you are Patrick's friend. B you are Patrick.

- Hi, how are you?
- Where are you?
- What's happening?
- What is your dad/mom/brother/the parrot doing?
- Great talking to you. See you later!

Writing

Time clauses – *right now/today/this week*

Today we're sailing close to the equator.
Right now she's watching for sharks.

6 Write the sentences using a time clause.

1 right now/I/write my diary
Right now I'm writing in my diary.
2 right now/mom/wear a bikini
3 this week/we/sailing near New Zealand
4 today/help my dad
5 right now/my mom/watch sharks

A webchat

7 Tell your friend what you are doing. Use the plan below to help you.

Research
Think about the things you usually do. Make notes. Use Patrick's diary to help you.

Draft
Write a draft.

emski	*Hi, how are you?*
bertie01	*Okay. What are you doing?*
emski	*Describe your situation. Where are you? What are you doing?*
bertie01	*Is your brother/sister there? What is he/she doing?*
emski	*Describe who is in your house and what they are doing.*

Check
Check your draft – are the time clauses correct? Write the final version.

5 Look again

Language

1 Write affirmative (+) and negative (-) sentences.

1 we watch/soccer on TV
+ *We are watching soccer on TV.*
- *We aren't watching soccer on TV.*
2 Corinne sunbathe/on the beach
3 your cell phone/ring
4 I talk to Celia/on my cell phone
5 I eat ice cream/right now

2 Write true short answers.

1 Are you using the computer right now?
No, I'm not.
2 Is your dad sleeping?
3 Is your brother/sister talking on the phone?
4 Are your parents sunbathing?
5 Is your teacher writing?
6 Are you eating?

3 Write the questions.

1 what/Corinne/do?
What is Corinne doing?
2 what/you/watch?
3 who/they/talk to?
4 why/Lucas/read a magazine?
5 who/she/listen to?
6 why/you/study English?

Vocabulary

4 Write the jobs.

1 *Farmers* work on a farm. (framers)
2 ________ usually wear a green uniform. (sdlieors)
3 ________ wear a white coat. (dcotros)
4 ________ write for a newspaper. (juonrlasits)
5 A ________ works in a school. (tceaher)
6 ________ help you with legal problems. (lwyares)
7 ________ work in very hot places. (fierhfgetirs)
8 ________ work with cars. (mscheianc)

5 Write the activities

Communication

6 Complete the conversation.

Mara Hi, [1] *it* 's Mara.
You [2] ______ Mara. [3] ______ ______ you?
Mara Great. What [4] ______ you ______ ?
You We're sunbathing.
Mara Awesome! Oops! I [5] ______ talk now.
You Thanks for [6] ______ .
Mara [7] ______ you later!
You [8] ______ !

Now you can…	☹ 😐 ☺
use present continuous – affirmative/negative (*ex 1*) – short answers (*ex 2*) – in questions (*ex 3*)	
name jobs (*ex 4*)	
name different activities (*ex 5*)	
chat on the phone (*ex 6*)	

Game

Follow these instructions:

- Use a die to move.
- In each square, follow the instruction or answer the question. If you are not correct, you go back one square.

6 Can you juggle?

Presentation **1** **Listen and read.**

Expressions

- It's easy!
- Not bad.
- Be careful!

Mark	Hey Joe! Can you juggle?
Joe	No, I can't. Can you?
Mark	Yes, I can. It's easy… two tomatoes…
Grandma	That's easy! Even I can do that! Watch…
Ellie	Wow! Even Grandma can juggle!
Grandma	Not bad, eh?
Mark	Yes, but two tomatoes and an onion?
Joe	Wow! Not bad. Hey, you *can* juggle!
Mark	… and two eggs…
Ellie	Be careful, Mark!
Mark	And another egg. Oops!
Ellie	Urgh!!
Mark	Are you hungry, Joe?
Joe	Actually, yes, I am. Why?
Mark	Because there's an omelet – on the floor!

Comprehension

2 True or false?

1 Joe can juggle.
2 Mark can juggle two tomatoes.
3 Mark can juggle two tomatoes, an onion and two eggs.
4 Joe is hungry.
5 The omelet is now on the table.
6 Grandma can juggle two tomatoes.

Vocabulary

3 Match the words with the pictures. Listen, check and repeat the words.

- cook an omelet
- juggle
- play the guitar
- play soccer (A)
- ride a horse
- run fast
- speak English
- swim
- use a cell phone

Listening

4 What can Ellie do? Write a tick (✓) or a cross (×) next to each picture.

Grammar bite

Can you … ?

Can you juggle three tomatoes?
Yes, I can./No, I can't.

Pronunciation

5 *Can or can't*? Listen and repeat the dialog.

Joe *Can you juggle?*
Ellie *Yes, I can.*

6 In pairs, ask and answer about the activities in exercise 3.

A: *Can you juggle?*
B: *Yes, I can./No, I can't.*

6 Language

1 Match the words with the activities.

- fly *d*
- run through walls
- stretch
- carry one ton
- make a force field
- become invisible

2 Read the text above and complete the table.

✓ = can × = can't ? = I don't know

Ability	Jack	Helen	Violet	Dash
run fast	×	×	×	✓
run through walls				
carry one ton				
fly				
stretch				
become invisible				
make a force field				

can – affirmative

I You He/She/It We/You/They	can	run.

3 Write the sentences in the correct order.

1. can/use a computer/I
   I can use a computer.
2. run fast/Dash/can
3. speak English/can/Helen and Jack
4. become invisible/Violet/can
5. swim/can/we
6. Elastigirl/stretch/can
7. play soccer/can/Filip
8. can/speak Italian/my friend

can – negative

I You He/She/It We/You/They	can't (can not)	run.

4 Rewrite these sentences as negatives.

1. Jack can fly.
   Jack can't fly.
2. He can run fast.
3. Helen can lift one ton.
4. Dash can become invisible.
5. Jack and Helen can run fast.
6. My sister can make a force field.
7. Joe can cook an omelet.
8. Mark can juggle.

5 Complete the sentences with the correct information.

1. Jack _*can*_ run through walls but he ______ fly.
2. Elastigirl ______ stretch her body but she ______ run fast.
3. Violet ______ run fast but she ______ become invisible.
4. Dash ______ become invisible but he ______ run very fast.

can – questions and short answers

Can	I you he/she/it we/you/they	run?	Yes, … can. No, … can't.

6 Write the questions and the correct short answers.

1. Mr. Incredible/lift one ton?
   Can Mr. Incredible lift one ton?
   Yes, he can.
2. he/fly?
3. Helen and Dash/run through walls?
4. Helen/stretch her body?
5. Violet/become invisible?
6. she/make a force field?
7. Dash/become invisible?
8. he/run fast?

6 Language

7 Look at the picture. Write the activities.

speak ride (x2) play swim run lift cook

A She *can't* fly.
B He ______ ______ the piano.
C They ______ ______ burgers.
D She ______ ______ Chinese.
E He ______ ______ one ton.
F They ______ ______ underwater.
G He ______ ______ a motorcycle.
H She ______ ______ a horse.
I He ______ ______ fast.

8 In pairs, point to the picture and check your answers.

A: *Can she fly?*
B: *Yes, she can./No, she can't.*

9 Listen and check your answers.

10 In pairs, each choose 5 activities you can do. Ask and answer. Write notes.

A: *Can you cook burgers?*
B: *Yes, I can.*

Extra

11 Make a poster for Frankie's Fabulous Fairground. Write about your partner.

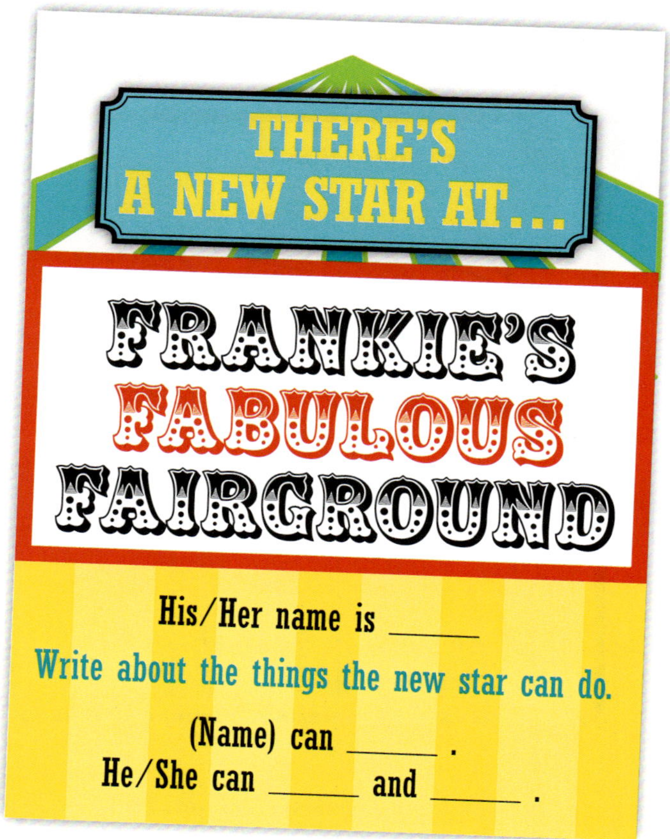

6 Communicate

Vocabulary

1 Match the words with the pictures. Listen, check and repeat the words.

- apple
- baked potato
- banana
- beans
- burger
- cheese
- chicken
- fish
- fries
- hot chocolate
- lemonade
- omelet
- orange
- orange juice
- pasta (A)
- peach
- pear
- peas
- salad

Order food

2 Listen and write the missing words.

Use *can* to ask for things politely.
Can I have a pizza?

Jenny	Hello.
Customer	Hi! [1] ______ ______ *have* a pizza, salad and fries, please?
Jenny	Sure. And to drink?
Customer	Can I [2] ______ orange juice, [3] ______ ?
Jenny	Pizza, [4] ______, and [5] ______, and [6] ______ ______. For here or to go?
Customer	For here, please.

3 In pairs, practice the dialog.

4 In pairs, A you work at a fast food restaurant. B, you are the customer. Choose a meal and order it!

A: ____________________.
B: *Hi! Can* ____________________?
A: *Sure.* ____________________ *drink?*
B: ____________________, *please.*
A: ____________________. *For here or to go?*
B: ____________________.

6 Skills

Future Star

We're at the TOP TV station. Six young people are in the American TV talent competition, Talented Kids. Tonight we talk to one of the young musicians, Orlando Rossi

Orlando's thirteen. He has long hair and he's from Santa Cruz in California. He has a violin but it's weird. What is it? It's an electric violin! "I can play the guitar and the violin," says Orlando. "I can also play rock music on the electric violin. It's different!" "Can you sing and dance too?" "No, I can't!

Orlando is the last kid on stage. The tune is *All Along the Watchtower* by Jimi Hendrix.

The music's fast and very good. Orlando can really play the violin! At the end of the show there is one winner – Orlando is the Talented Kid. After the show Orlando is hot and he's really hungry. "Can we eat something now? A pizza?" **Orlando's a star but he's also an ordinary kid.**

Reading

Words you need

a competition
talented
weird
on stage

1 Look at the picture and title. What do you think this text is about?

2 Read about *Talented Kids* and answer the questions.

1 What is "Talented Kids"?
2 How old is Orlando?
3 Where is he from?
4 What instruments can he play?
5 What instrument does he have in the TV show?
6 Who is today's Talented Kid?

Listening

3 Listen to the interview. Who is Pavarotti?

4 Listen again. Choose the correct answer.

1 Joss King is from a radio/TV station.
2 Nicola is thirteen/fourteen.
3 Her favorite music is jazz/rock.
4 Nicola can play the guitar/piano.
5 She has a little brother/sister.
6 Lucy can play the violin/dance and sing.
7 Pavarotti can/can't sing.

Speaking

5 You are a DJ. Interview your partner on the radio. Take turns to ask the questions.

- I'm ______ and this is Radio 85.5 FM.
- How old are you?
- And what's your favorite music?
- Can you play the piano or the guitar?
- What other things can you do?
- Do you have any brothers or sisters?
- Is he/she talented too?

Writing

Linking sentences (1) – *and/but*

*I can sing **and** I can dance.*
*I can sing **but** I can't dance.*

6 Connect these sentences with *and* or *but*.

1 I can swim. I can ride a bike
I can swim and I can ride a bike.
2 I can play the guitar. I can't sing.
3 He can sing. He can juggle.
4 Nicci can speak English. She can't speak Italian.
5 I can't ride a horse. I can ride a bike. I can skateboard.

An informal letter

7 Write a letter to a friend about what you can and can't do.

Research
Read Orlando's note below. What does he talk about?

Hello,
My name's Orlando Rossi. I'm thirteen years old. I am from California. I can play the guitar and the violin but I can't play the piano. I can't sing and dance and I can't ride a horse.
Bye,
Orlando

Draft
Write a draft.

Hello,
My name's...
Bye,

Check
Check your draft – are the linking words correct? Write a final version.

6 Look again

Language

1 Write what they *can* and *can't* do.

Paul

1 Speak English ✓
He can speak English.
2 Speak Chinese ✗
3 Ride a horse ✗
4 Use a computer ✓

Anita and Robin

1 Speak English ✗
They can't speak English.
2 Speak Chinese ✓
3 Ride a horse ✓
4 Use a computer ✗

2 Write the questions and the correct short answers.

1 Paul/speak English?
Can Paul speak English?
Yes, he can.
2 Anita and Robin/use a computer?
3 Paul/ride a horse?
4 Anita and Robin/ride a horse?
5 Paul/speak Chinese?

Vocabulary

3 Complete the phrases.

1 *r u n* fast
2 _ _ _ _ underwater
3 _ _ _ _ the piano
4 _ _ _ a cell phone
5 _ _ _ _ _ English
6 _ _ _ _ an omelet
7 _ _ _ _ a motorbike
8 _ _ _ _ _ _ with tomatoes and eggs

4 Write the words.

Communication

5 Write the dialog in a cafeteria.

Waiter Hello.
You Hello. Can ______ burger and fries, please?
Waiter Sure. And to drink?
You _________ lemonade, please?
Waiter For here ______ ?

Now you can…	☹😐☺
use the verb *can* – affirmative/negative (*ex 1*) – questions/answers (*ex 2*)	
use activity verbs (*ex 3*)	
name food/drink (*ex 4*)	
order food (*ex 5*)	

Breakfast in America: Decisions, Decisions!

Americans don't make breakfast easy.

It's not easy to order breakfast in the USA. First, Americans love eggs for breakfast, but they like eggs in many different ways – and not just in omelets. A typical question waiters ask in American restaurants is "How do you like your eggs?" And there are many options. "Scrambled" is a very common option, with eggs all "mixed up." "Fried" is also a popular option. But there are many others!

scrambled eggs

fried eggs

Popular egg options in the USA.

After you order eggs, you think, *Good – I'm finished*! No. You're not finished. The waiter/waitress can also ask you about bread: "What kind of toast?" More decisions! The options are many, but they include white bread, bagels, and English muffins!

Finally, it's time for coffee. You can order a normal coffee (also called "house coffee"), but more and more people want different coffees, like "latte" (espresso coffee with milk), "mocha" (coffee with chocolate and milk), and the popular "americano" (espresso coffee with water).

bagel

English muffins

a typical coffee menu

1 Read about breakfast in the USA and answer the questions.

1 What kind of food is "scrambled?"
2 What kind of food is "toast?"
3 What kind of bread does not have a photo in the article?
4 What is "house coffee?"
5 What two coffees have milk in them?
6 What is the name of the espresso with water in it?

2 Same or different?

1 How about in your country? Do people eat eggs for breakfast? Are there many options?
2 What are the most typical foods for breakfast in your country? What different options are there?

7 Look at that giraffe!

Presentation

1 Listen and read.

Expressions
- Don't be silly!
- See?
- Come on!
- Oh yeah.

Ellie	Wow! Look at that giraffe! If you call it, it comes to you.
Mark	Here, giraffe! Here, boy!
Joe	It's not a dog, Mark. It wants food.
Ellie	Give it some peanuts.
Joe	Peanuts? Are you kidding? Come on – it's not an elephant!
Ellie	Mrs. Murray, do you have any food for the giraffe?
Mrs. Murray	We can get some giraffe food at the store there.
Joe	Thanks, Mom. Here… see?
Ellie	Cool.
Joe	If you give him food, he stays. He loves it.
Mark	How do you know it's a "he?"
Joe	It's a he. His name is Mark.
Ellie	Ha ha!
Mark	Hey! If he wants to drink, I have some water here!
Ellie	Don't be silly! He doesn't have hands!
Mark	Oh yeah.

Comprehension

2 **Circle the correct answer.**

1 Peanuts *are / are not* good food for giraffes.
2 They are with *Ellie's mom and dad / Joe's mom and dad*.
3 They can buy *giraffe food / peanuts* at the store.
4 The giraffe comes *if you call it / if you give it food*.
5 The giraffe is a *girl / boy*.

Vocabulary

3 **Match the words with the pictures. Listen, check and repeat the words.**

parrot
cat
chicken
cow
dog
duck
eagle
elephant
giraffe
goldfish
horse
lion (A)
monkey
rabbit
snake

4 **In pairs, listen and identify the animals from the sounds. Then check together.**

Pronunciation

5 **/dʒ/ or /tʃ/? Listen and choose the sound you hear. Then listen and repeat.**

ginger **ch**eese **j**uggle **j**uice
choose **ch**air **g**iraffe **ch**icken

6 **Write the names of the animals above in the correct column.**

In the wild	On a farm	At home
giraffe	*horse*	*cat*

Learning Tip
Remembering vocabulary
Associate new words with a person, place or thing.
A giraffe lives in the wild.

7 Language

Countable and uncountable nouns

We can count some things.
These are countable nouns.

We can't count some things.
These are uncountable nouns.

+ *some* – affirmative

Countable nouns can be singular or plural.
Use *some* with plurals.

I have a peanut.
I have **some** peanuts.

Uncountable nouns can't be plural.

I have **some** sugar.

1 Can you count the objects? Write the words in the correct column.

Countable	Uncountable
	milk

2 Write the correct form of the noun.

1 I have some (peanut) for the giraffe.
I have some peanuts for the giraffe.
2 There are some (apple) in the car.
3 There are some (banana) too.
4 Hey! It can have some (water).
5 I have some (peach).
6 Water? I have some (lemonade).
7 There's some (sugar) here.
8 I have some (orange).

3 Complete the sentences with *a* or *some*.

1 There's *some* lemonade in the fridge.
2 I have ________ computer in my room.
3 There's ________ sugar in the cupboard.
4 There's ________ pen in my bag.
5 There's ________ food on the table.
6 Can I have ________ orange juice, please?
7 He has ________ milk.
8 Mark has ________ banana.

–/? *Any* – negative and questions

Countable and uncountable nouns use *any* in negative sentences and questions.

Countable

I don't have **any** peanuts.
Do you have **any** peanuts?

Uncountable

I don't have **any** sugar.
Do you have **any** sugar?

? *How much/How many…?*

Countable

How **many** bananas are there?

Uncountable

How **much** salt is there?

We use *how many* to ask about *countable* things and we use *how much* to ask about *uncountable* things.

4 **Complete the dialog in the store. Write *some* or *any*.**

Customer	Do you have [1] *any* milk?
Assistant	I don't have [2]_______ milk, but I have [3]_______ water.
Customer	Do you have [4]_______ apples?
Assistant	I don't have [5]_______ apples, but I have [6]_______ peaches.
Customer	Hmmm… okay, can I have [7]_______ water and [8]_______ peaches?

5 **Listen to the dialog between the zoo keeper and the person working at the store. Complete the shopping list.**

Elephant food
- Cakes (*48*)
- Peaches (_______)
- Sugar (_______)
- Bananas (_______)
- Water (_______)
- Apples (_______)
- Milk (_______)

Extra

6 **Write *How much* or *How many* in the conversation. Then listen to check.**

Keeper	Can I have some cakes for the elephants?
Assistant	Of course. [1] *How many* ?
Keeper	Forty-eight. And some peaches.
Assistant	[2]_________ peaches?
Keeper	Twenty-seven. And some sugar.
Assistant	[3]_________ sugar?
Keeper	Three kilos. Some bananas.
Assistant	[4]_________ bananas?
Keeper	Seventy-five. Some water.
Assistant	Some water. [5]_________ water?
Keeper	Twenty liters. Oh, some apples.
Assistant	OK. [6]_________ apples?
Keeper	Ninety-six. And some milk.
Assistant	[7]_________ milk?
Keeper	Forty-five liters.

7 Language

"Zero" conditional – affirmative

You can use the zero conditional to talk about *cause* → *effect*.

Cause	Effect
You call the giraffe. →	It comes to you.
You give him food. →	He stays.

Zero Conditional

you call the giraffe, it comes.

you give him food, he stays.

"Zero" conditional + imperative

You can mix an "If" clause with an imperative.

7 Match a cause to an effect.

1 If I do my homework at night,
2 If you exercise,
3 If Nick plays,
4 If it rains,
5 If you use a calculator,

___ I want to go to sleep.
___ it's easy to do math homework.
___ the team always wins.
___ we stay home and watch TV.
___ you feel well.

If you can read this, thank a TEACHER.

8 Write your school rules.

ask be give raise say share use

School Rules

1 If you arrive late, ________ sorry to the class.

2 If you work in pairs, ________ polite.

3 If you don't know a word, ________ a dictionary.

4 If you have a snack, ________ with friends.

5 If you have a question, ________ your hand.

6 If you need to use Portuguese, ________ the teacher first.

7 If you find a lost object, ________ it to the teacher.

7 Communicate

Vocabulary

1 Match signs to the words. Listen, check and repeat the words.

Be careful!
Don't turn left
Don't turn right
Go straight ahead
Go!
Stop! (A)
Turn left
Turn right

Give instructions

2 Listen to Joe's mom. Follow the route on the map. Which gate do they use to leave the safari park?

3 Listen again and complete these instructions.

Mom OK go! Now [1] *turn* left.
Dad Here?
Mom Yes.... [2] __________ ahead. Oh, it's red.
Dad Stop?
Mom Of course! [3] ________ it's red, you [4] ________!

4 In pairs, decide what you want to see. Give instructions to your partner. B, follow A's instructions. Where do you arrive?

A: *OK... go straight ahead.*
B: *This way?*
A: *No, if you go that way you go to the elephants. Now turn right.*
B: *Turn right. OK.*

7 Skills

SPECIAL PETS

I'm Janie and this is Honey. Honey is my best friend and also my pet. She has an orange and white harness. Why? Because she's a Guide Dog for the Blind. I'm blind, but Honey can see. Some of my instructions are simple: "Go," "Stop," "Turn left," and "Turn right." Honey sees traffic — if she stops, I stop! She can understand instructions because she's very intelligent. Honey is with me all the time. At school, please don't talk to Honey because she's at work. Come and play with Honey at home. If you give her cheese, she loves it — it's her favorite!

Reading

Words you need

harness
blind
instructions
cheetah
fur
wild

1 Look at the pictures. What do you think the texts are about?

2 Read the texts. Write a ✓ in the correct box.

	Honey	Rocky
1 intelligent		
2 shy		
3 can understand instructions		
4 favorite food – chicken		
5 favorite food – cheese		
6 doesn't have a mother		

3 True or false?

1 Honey is blind.
2 Honey can speak English.
3 Guide dogs for the blind have red harnesses.
4 You can talk to Honey at school.
5 Rocky is a young cheetah.
6 Amanda can touch Rocky.
7 Rocky isn't really a pet.
8 Cheetahs are wild animals.

I'm Amanda from the Cheetah Project in South Africa, and this is Rocky. He's a young cheetah but he doesn't have a mother. Cheetahs are very shy animals – if you come close it hides or runs. But I can sit very near Rocky and I can touch his fur. He isn't really a pet. He's a wild animal. One day he can go back to the wild. This is Rocky's favorite food… it's chicken! Come and see Rocky but be careful. If you shout, run, or take flash photos, he doesn't like it!

Listening

4 **Listen and number the pets.**

5 **Listen again and answer the questions.**

1 How old is the monkey?
2 What is the chicken's favorite place?
3 Can Dave's parrot fly?
4 How old is the crocodile?

Speaking

6 **In pairs, ask questions about your favorite animal.**

A: *What's your favorite animal?*
B: *Monkeys.*
A: *Why?*
B: *They're intelligent.*

Writing

Linking sentences (2) – *because*

A: *Why is he your favorite pet?*
B: *I like my pet **because** he's friendly.*

7 **Answer the questions with *because*.**

1 Why is she your best friend? (friendly)
Because she's very friendly.
2 Why are you hungry? (any food)
3 Why does Honey have a harness? (guide dog)
4 Why can't I play with Honey? (at work)
5 Why can't I take photos of Rocky? (scared)
6 Why isn't Rocky in the wild? (a mother)

My pet

8 **Write about a favorite pet.**

Research
Think about your pet. Do you have any pictures of him/her?

Draft
Write a draft.

Introduce your pet.
My favorite animal is a… because…
His/her name's…
He/She's my pet/a friend's pet
Describe your pet
(S)he's… and (s)he has…

Give instructions for the pet's care
Give him/her some water.
Don't give milk to this animal.
If you touch her/him, she purrs.
If it rains, he/she likes to stay inside.

Conclusion
He/She's my favorite animal because…

Check
Check your draft – have you used *because* correctly? Write the final version.

7 Look again

Language

1 Write countable (C) or uncountable (U).

1 apple	*C*	6 milk	____
2 banana	____	7 orange	____
3 burger	____	8 peach	____
4 cake	____	9 sugar	____
5 lemonade	____	10 water	____

2 Write *some* or *any*.

1. I have *some* peanuts.
2. Do you have ________ milk?
3. She doesn't have ________ food.
4. There are ________ sausages here.
5. There aren't ________ fries.
6. Is there ________ cheese?

3 Write *how much* or *how many*.

1. *How many* apples are there?
2. ____________ water do you have?
3. ____________ milk is there?
4. ____________ burgers are there?
5. ____________ pizzas are there?
6. ____________ rabbits are there?

Vocabulary

4 Write the words.

5 Write the directions.

1 *Stop!* 2 ________ 3 ________ 4 ________

5 ________ 6 ________ 7 ________ 8 ________

Communication

6 Follow the arrows and complete the directions.

Fred OK, go [1] *straight ahead* and then turn [2] ________ .
Janet OK, and then…?
Fred Go [3] ________ ahead again and then [4] ________ ________.
Janet OK, here?
Fred Yes. Now, [5] ________ ________ again and go [6] ________ ________.
Now [7] ________ and you are there.

Now you can…	☹ 😐 ☺
use un/countable nouns – identify the difference (*ex 1*) – with *some/any* (*ex 2*) – questions (*ex 3*)	
name animals (*ex 4*)	
label directions (*ex 5*)	
give directions on a map (*ex 6*)	

Game

Follow these instructions:

- Use a die to move.
- In each square, follow the instruction or answer the question. If you are not correct, you go back one square.

8 I hate cleaning

Presentation 1 **Listen and read.**

Mark	Mom! Where's my red T-shirt?
Mom	Don't shout! I always put your clean clothes on your bed.
Mark	Can you see my T-shirt, Ellie?
Ellie	No way! This room is a disaster area!
Mark	No, it isn't!
Ellie	Oh, Mark! You never clean your room!
Mark	Ellie, you like cleaning your room. I hate cleaning but I usually put the clean clothes near the bed.
Ellie	Great! So where are they?
Mark	Umm... maybe they're under the bed.
Ellie	What's that? In Clyde's basket?
Mark	Hey, Ellie! Don't wake him up!
Ellie	Here's your T-shirt.
Mark	And my socks! Thanks Clyde.
Ellie	And here's my pink top! Oh no — it smells horrible!

Comprehension

2 Choose the correct answer.

1 Mark and Ellie are in a) Ellie's b) Mark's room.
2 His mom always puts his clean clothes a) under b) on the bed.
3 Mark wants to find a) his T-shirt b) his socks.
4 Mark a) cleans b) doesn't clean his room.
5 Mark's T-shirt is a) near the door b) in Clyde's basket.
6 Ellie is a) angry b) happy about her pink top.

Vocabulary

3 Match the words with the pictures. Listen, check and repeat the words.

boots
bracelet
cap
dress
earrings
hat
jacket (A)
jeans
necklace
pants
sandals
scarf
shirt
shorts
skirt
sneakers
socks
sweatshirt
top
T-shirt
watch

4 Can you find 8 items of clothing in the photo of Mark's bedroom?

A: *There's a jacket.*
B: *Where?*
A: *On the door.*

Learning Tip
Remembering vocabulary
In your notebook use wordwebs to store your vocabulary.

hats — clothes — shoes
cap (hats) · boots (shoes)

8 Language

Hi! I'm Pat. At work, I always wear a uniform because I'm a mailman. I sometimes wear a cap. I usually wear boots, but I sometimes wear sneakers. I never wear sandals or shorts. I always have a big blue bag and it's usually full of mail!

Adverbs of frequency

1 Read about Pat. Circle the adverbs and answer the questions.

a Do the adverbs come before or after the verb?

b Which verb is different?

2 Complete the sentences.

1 Pat *always* wears a ________.
2 He ________ wears a cap.
3 He sometimes wears ______ on his feet.
4 He never wears ________ or ________.
5 He ________ has a big blue bag.

Adverbs of frequency – position

3 Complete the sentences with the correct adverb of frequency.

1 Pat (100%) *always* wears a uniform.
2 He (0%) ________ wears sandals.
3 Mr. Murray (0%) ________ goes out.
4 I (25%) ________ play computer games after school.
5 My dad (75%) ________ plays soccer on Saturday.
6 I (25%) ________ do my homework on the bus.
7 Ellie (0%) ________ cleans her room.
8 Katie (75%) ________ puts her clean clothes in the closet.
9 I (50%) ________ put my dirty socks on the floor.

4 Rewrite these sentences with the adverb in the correct position.

1 Mark puts his dirty clothes near the door. (always)
Mark always puts his dirty clothes near the door.
2 At a party, I wear my favorite shirt. (usually)
3 I ride my bike to school. (never)
4 I take a shower in the morning. (always)
5 We visit my grandparents on Sunday. (sometimes)
6 I play chess with my dad on Sunday. (often)
7 My brother takes his cell phone to school. (usually)
8 We watch TV before school. (sometimes)

This is me on the weekend. I like playing tennis. I like wearing shorts or jeans, a T-shirt and sneakers. Hmm, my sneakers are usually smelly! I don't like getting up early! I usually get up at ten.

Adding *-ing* to verbs

- do → do**ing**
- dance → danc**ing**
- swim → swim**ming**
  get → get**ting**

Adverbs of frequency – *to be*

5 Write the sentences in the correct order.

1 sneakers/my/usually/smelly/are
My sneakers are usually smelly.
2 hungry/am/always/I
3 sings/often/dog/my
4 sometimes/on/the/bus/do/I/my homework
5 Mrs. Trent/friendly/is/usually
6 in school/my cell phone/use/I/never
7 on the weekend/get up/I/usually/at/ten o'clock
8 classroom/hot/my/is/sometimes
9 late/often/my/is/boyfriend
10 cat/on/sofa/our/usually/the/sleeps

6 Write the *-ing* form of these verbs.

1 do *doing*
2 wear ________
3 use ________
4 dance ________
5 swim ________
6 get ________
7 clean ________
8 cook ________

7 Write the correct form of the verb in parentheses.

1 Pat likes *wearing* (wear) shorts.
2 He likes ________ (play) tennis.
3 He likes ________ (get up) at ten o'clock.
4 I like ________ (go out) on Saturday.
5 My brother likes ________ (clean) his room.
6 I like ________ (walk) to school.
7 She likes ________ (play) the piano.
8 I like ________ (get up) in the morning.
9 We like ________ (play) volleyball.

8 Rewrite the sentences in exercise 7 as negatives.

1 *Pat doesn't like wearing shorts.*

8 Language

9 In pairs, write about you then ask your partner.

How often do you…?

1 … play tennis after school.
I sometimes play tennis after school.
2 … clean your room.
3 … eat breakfast in bed.
4 … meet friends on the weekend.
5 … help your mom.
6 … wear a skirt to school.
7 … do homework in front of the TV.
8 … have a cold shower in the morning.

10 Listen to Ben and Jess and complete the sentences.

1 Ben never wears *black* *shoes*.
2 He always wears ________ .
3 At a party Ben usually wears ____________.
4 At school Jess always wears a white ________ .
5 She hates wearing ______________ .
6 With friends she usually wears ________ and a ________.
7 She never wears ________.

11 In pairs, ask and answer about your clothes.

1 What/usually wear at home?
– at school?
– at a party?
2 What/your favorite shoes?
3 What clothes/hate wearing?

A: *What clothes do you usually wear at home?*
B: *I usually wear…*

Extra

12 Draw 2 quick pictures of you.

13 Write a description for each picture.

This is me in my normal clothes.
I usually wear…
This is me in my party clothes.
I like wearing…

8 Communicate

Vocabulary

1 Match the activities and the words. Listen, check and repeat the words.

- clean
- clean my room
- cook
- do the dishes (A)
- do the laundry
- do the shopping
- help my grandmother
- make my bed
- take care of the pet
- take out the trash

Grammar bite

love → hate

☺ *I love cooking.*
I like doing the laundry.
I don't mind cleaning.
I don't like doing the shopping.
☹ *I hate cleaning my room.*

Talk about helping at home

2 In pairs, point at a picture and ask the question.

A: *Do you like taking out the trash?*
B: *No, I hate taking out the trash/I don't mind…*

3 Do a survey about you and 2 friends. Complete the first column about you.

A: *How often do you do the laundry?*
B: *I never do the laundry!*

Activities	Me	Friend 1	Friend 2
do laundry	*sometimes*	*never*	…

Pronunciation

4 /ʊ/ or /uː/? Listen and choose the sound you hear. Then listen and repeat.

look food book cook cool
foot moon tooth

FASHION UPDATE

TWO SIDES OF *fashion*

This is Selina. She's sixteen and she lives in Los angeles. On the weekend she usually wears designer dresses, shoes and expensive earrings. She's a model.

"I love wearing expensive clothes," she says. "I always work on the weekend, so it's OK for school. A session is about seven or eight hours. The other girls are friendly and I earn $60 a day. It's fun!"

Are there any boring times? "I don't like waiting in studios so I often do my homework. I hate the traveling... I usually travel about 300 kilometers on the weekend – but my mom is always with me, so I'm never lonely."

My T-shirt

Anthony's fourteen. He lives in Sweden and he's a clothes designer. His parents are designers and he often helps them. They all work at home.

Anthony goes to school, so he usually works on the weekend. "My mom and dad design clothes for adults, but I like designing cool and funny teenage clothes. Look at this awesome T-shirt. It says 'Outside the graphics are not so cool".

"I really like designing clothes. It's fun and I can earn about $50 for a good design."

Reading

1 Look at the title and the pictures. What do you think the texts are about?

Words you need

- session
- lonely
- designer
- awesome

2 Read the texts. Complete the table.

	Selina	Anthony
1 How old are they?		
2 Where do they live?		
3 What work do they do?		
4 When do they work?		
5 How much money do they earn?		
6 Do they like the work?		
7 Why?/Why not?		

Listening

3 Listen to Louise talking about one of the days in the week. What day is it?

4 Listen again, and answer the questions.

1 What time does she get up?
2 What does she do in the morning?
3 What clothes does she wear?
4 What does she do on Saturday evening?
5 What does she not like about Saturday?

Speaking

5 In pairs, ask and answer the questions in exercise 4 about you.

A: *What time do you get up?*
B: *I usually get up at…*

Writing

Linking sentences (4) – *so*

My mom is always with me, **so** *I'm never lonely.*

He goes to school, **so** *he usually works on the weekend.*

6 Write sentences with *so*, in the correct order.

1 I leave home at 8:00. School starts at 8:30.
School starts at 8:30, so I leave home at 8:00.
2 There isn't a bus to school. I walk.
3 My friend lives in the same street. I usually walk with her.
4 I take sandwiches. There isn't a café at school.
5 I sometimes play soccer after school. I'm in the soccer club.
6 School finishes at 3:30. I'm usually home at 4:00.

A magazine article

7 Describe what your friends like wearing on the weekend.

Research
Talk to your friends. Make notes. Collect photos or draw pictures.

Draft
Write a draft.

Introduce your friends
Megan is twelve and she is… Matt is thirteen,…
Describe his/her clothes
On Saturday Megan usually wears… in the morning. In the afternoon she sometimes plays soccer, so she wears…

Check
Check your draft – are the linking words correct? Write the final version.

8 Look again

Language

1 Write the correct adverb of frequency.

1 She *sometimes* (50%) wears a bracelet.
2 I ________ (75%) walk to school.
3 He ________ (0%) does his homework.
4 We ________ (25%) visit our grandmother.
5 They ________ (100%) go to the park after school.
6 I ________ (0%) play soccer.
7 She ________ (100%) uses a pink pen.

2 Circle the correct word.

1 (I'm always)/I always am late.
2 She often is/She's often here at nine o'clock.
3 They're sometimes/They sometimes are early.
4 My mom usually is/is usually at the office at six.
5 You're never/You never are here.
6 My dogs are always/always are hungry.
7 Usually we're/We're usually in bed at eleven.

3 Write the correct form of the verbs.

1 I like *going* (go) to bed.
2 I hate ________ (get up).
3 I like ________ (have) breakfast.
4 I don't mind ________ (walk) to school.
5 I don't like ________ (do) my homework.
6 I like ________ (visit) my cousin.
7 He likes ________ (ride) horses.
8 I don't mind ________ (take care of) the dogs.

Vocabulary

4 Complete the phrases.

1 *do* the dishes
2 ______ my room
3 ______ my pet
4 ______ the trash
5 ______ my bed

5 Write the words.

Communication

6 Answer the questions.

1 Do you like doing the dishes?
2 Do you like cooking?
3 Do you like cleaning your room?
4 Do you like making your bed?
5 Do you like taking out the trash?

Now you can…	☹ 😐 ☺
use adverbs of frequency – in sentences (*ex 1*) – in the correct order (*ex 2*)	
talk about likes/dislikes (*ex 3*)	
name household chores (*ex 4*)	
name clothes (*ex 5*)	
talk about chores (*ex 6*)	

Culture spot

Fashion creativity in Iran

Iranian women are very creative. Men can wear "normal" clothes, but the rules for women are different. In public, Iranian women always wear a "hijab" on their heads, a kind of scarf. It's the law in Iran. The "hijab" usually covers the head and the hair of the women, but some women are creative and they sometimes wear the front of their hair *outside* the "hijab", in many different ways.

Iranian women usually can't show their jewelry in public, like bracelets, necklaces, and earrings, but they can wear some accessories, so sometimes they wear really nice and interesting (and expensive!) sunglasses, watches and bags to show their fashion sense.

Another item of clothing Iranian women love is shoes. There are some size and shape limits, but they can be any color! It's a great way to express their personality and style.

Finally, it's true that Iranian women never go out in public without their hijab: they always have their hair covered. But there are no rules about color and fabric. Iranian women learn to wear their hijabs in all different kinds of ways.

Young Iranian women and their fashion sense.

Showing off accessories in a shopping mall.

A woman choosing a shoe in Tehran, Iran.

A young woman and her *hijab*.

1 Read the text.

1 What do women in Iran wear on their heads?
2 What kind of clothes do men in Iran wear?
3 What accessories do women like to show in public?
4 What are the rules about the color and fabric of hijabs?

2 Same or different?

- Do you have rules in your country about what women and men can/can't wear?
- What about at your school? What rules are there about what you can/can't wear?

Unit 1 Packing up!

Key Words

skateboard	toothbrush
video game	sunglasses
book	clothes
umbrella	mirror
magazine	brush
cell phone	shoes
keys	

Extra words

camera
tablet
documents

Look and learn

1 **Find the key words in the picture.**

A: *Where are the keys?*
B: *They are here.*

2 **Point to the picture and say the word in English.**

3 **Talk to a partner.**

A: *What is this?*
B: *This is an umbrella.*

4 **Write the new words in your notebook.**

Unit 2 Rooms

Key Words

bathroom	stove
bedroom	cupboard
dining room	desk
hall	fridge
kitchen	lamp
living room	painting
bed	couch
chair	

Extra words

study	door
floor	wall
stairs	rug

Look and learn

1 Make incomplete sentences to your partner about the places in the picture.

A: *I sleep in the ...*
B: *...bedroom!*

2 Point to the picture and say the names of the rooms in English.

3 Talk to a partner.

A: *Where is the fridge?*
B: *It is in the kitchen.*

4 Write the new words in your notebook.

Unit 3 Parts of the body

Key Words

arm	head
beard	leg
ears	mustache
eyes	mouth
face	nose
foot	tooth
hand	

Extra words

bone	chest
ankle	eyebrow

Look and learn

1 **Point and ask a partner.**

A: *What is it?*
B: *It's a leg.*

2 **Work with a partner. Point at the parts of the body your partner says.**

A: *Mustache.*
B: *Here.*

3 **Drawing. Work with a partner and find out what your partner is drawing.**

A: *Is it a leg?*
B: *No, it isn't. Try again. / Yes, it is!*

Unit 4 Routine

Key Words

do the homework	take guitar lessons
get dressed	have breakfast
get up	have lunch
go to bed	have dinner
go to school	play video game
take a shower	play soccer

Extra words

visit my grandparents
watch a movie
play with a pet

Look and learn

1 **Point and ask a partner.**

A: *What is he doing here?*
B: *He is playing the guitar.*

2 **Point and say the names of the activities.**

3 **Talk to a partner. Ask about the activities.**

A: *Is he playing the piano?*
B: *No, he's not. He's playing the guitar.*

4 **Write the new words in your notebook.**

Unit 5 Occupations

Key Words

doctor	mechanic	soldier
soccer player	nurse	student
farmer	police officer	teacher
firefighter	receptionist	
journalist	lawyer	

Extra words

vet painter singer salesperson

Look and learn

1 **Ask about the occupations.**

A: *What is his occupation?*
B: *He is a police officer.*

2 **Point and confirm the jobs.**

A: *Is she a doctor?*
B: *No, she's not. She's a nurse.*

3 **Guessing game. Choose an occupation. Help your partner to guess it.**

A: *Is it a man or a woman?*
B: *It's a woman.*
A: *Does she work at a hospital?*
B: *Yes, she does.*
A: *Is she the nurse?*
B: *Yes, she is!*

4 **Write the new words in your notebook.**

Unit 6 Food

Key Words

apple	fish	pasta
baked potato	fries	peach
banana	cocoa	pear
beans	lemonade	peas
burger	omelet	salad
cheese	orange	
chicken	orange juice	

Extra words

sausages milk water fried egg

Look and learn

1 **Locate the key words in the illustration with a partner.**

A: *Where are the bananas?*
B: *They are here.*

2 **Point and ask.**

A: *Are these bananas?*
B: *Yes, they are. / No, they aren't. They are apples.*

3 **Memory game. Look at the illustration for a minute. Then close your books. Ask questions about it.**

A: *Is there a burger?*
B: *Yes, there is.*

4 **Write the new words in your notebook.**

Unit 7 Animals

Key Words

parrot	duck	horse
cat	eagle	lion
chicken	elephant	monkey
cow	giraffe	rabbit
dog	golden fish	snake

Extra words

bear	cheetah	hamster
fish	tiger	

Look and learn

1 **Identify the key words in the illustration.**

A: *What is it?*
B: *It's a chicken.*

2 **Point and say the names of the animals.**

3 **Talk to a partner about the animals.**

B: *Do you like snakes?*
A: *Yes, I do. / No, I don't!*

4 **Play hangman. Choose a key word from the list.**

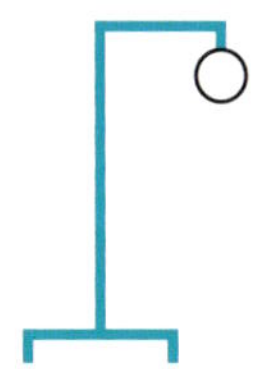

S _ _ _ _ _

Unit 8 Chores

Key Words

clean my room	make the bed
cook	take care of the pet
do the dishes	take out the trash
do the laundry	vacuum
go shopping	sweep

Extra words

dust	take a walk

Look and learn

1 Identify the key words in the illustration.

A: *What is it?*
B: *Cooking.*

2 Point and check the activities with a partner.

A: *This is cooking, right?*
B: *Yes, it is. / No, it isn't. It's 'doing the dishes'.*

3 Talk to a partner about the activities. Ask as many questions as possible.

A: *Do you like taking out the trash?*
B: *No, I don't. But I do it.*
A: *When do you take out the trash?*
B: *On Wednesdays and Fridays.*

4 Write the new words in your notebook.

A job for superheroes?

Cast

TV crew
presenter
camera operator
director
director's assistant
3 reporters
studio audience

Superherœs

Lightning Boy (or Girl)
Strong Man (or Woman)
Elastico
Mystery Girl (or Boy)

Scene 1: The studio

[Director checks the TV show: the presenter is sitting looking into the camera.]

Director Is everyone ready?

[Director's assistant holds up a clapperboard. It's got, 'A job for superheroes' on it.]

Director Three, two, one… Action!
Presenter Good afternoon. Today we are talking about a serious problem in our school. To solve this problem, we have some special guests. Can we meet our guests, please?

[Studio audience claps. Lightning Boy comes in through the door.]

Presenter Thank you for coming, and your name is…
Lightning Boy I am Lightning Boy. I can run really fast and I can do lots of things really quickly. I am a really, really fast superhero.
Presenter Welcome to the show. And our next guest is….

[Studio audience claps: Strong Man comes in through the door.]

Presenter And what's your name, please?

Strong Man I am Strong Man. I can lift one ton and I can carry it for three kilometers. And this is my friend Elastico…

[Studio audience claps. Elastico comes in through the door.]

Elastico Hi everyone! I can stretch my body. My arms are five meters long and I am really elastic!
Presenter Thank you! And our final guest is,… Mystery Girl.

[Other superheroes look confused.]

Lightning Boy Mystery Girl? Who's mystery girl?

[A small girl comes through the door – very normal, no obvious superpowers.]

Presenter Er… Mystery Girl. What's your superpower?
Mystery Girl I can't tell you. It's a mystery.
Presenter *[to the audience]* Er… OK. Well, why are we here? What's the big problem? Why do we need superheroes?

[Presenter reaches forward and lifts the blanket off the table. Under the blanket is a lot of rubbish – crisp packets, plastic bottles, pieces of paper, a pizza box.]

Presenter And the answer is… trash! Our school is full of trash and we can't get rid of it! Can you solve this problem, superheroes?
Lightning Boy This is a job for… Lightning Boy! I can solve your problem! Watch me in action!

[He runs out of the door.]

Strong Man … and me too! Come on Elastico! Let's use our superpowers!

[They run out of the door. Mystery Girl is still sitting by the table. She looks at the audience, shrugs and walks slowly out of the door.]

Presenter And now we go to our outside reporters – they are reporting from the action.
Director Camera crew! Follow those superheroes! And where's my assistant? Who is Mystery Girl? Find out now!

Scene 2: The playground

[Reporters 1, 2 and 3 report on the action – very loud, like a report on a race. Superheroes mime the activities.]

Reporter 1 The superheroes are moving into action. Lightning Boy is running around the playground. He's picking up lots of paper and putting it in the trash can. He's moving really fast…
Reporter 2 Strong Man is fantastic! He's carrying ten trash cans in one hand – and twelve cans in the other hand!
Reporter 3 Elastico is stretching her arms. She's picking up all the trash by the school gate. Now she's running towards Lightning Boy and Strong Man… oh no! They're going to…

CRASH!

Scene 3: The studio

Presenter And the result from our superheroes is… nothing. They can't solve the problem of our trash! What can we do?
Mystery Girl Er… I have an idea.
Presenter Oh… what?
Mystery Girl Picking up trash isn't a job for superheroes. It's a job for everyone – for you *[pointing at the audience]* and you… and you!
Presenter Of course! You're right. We can all solve this problem together. But what is your superpower?
Mystery Girl I'm, er… intelligent. Intelligence is the only superpower you need.

Alien visit

Cast

Reporter, Janey Jabber (JJ)
President, Mr. President
General Panic (GP)
Boy, Frank
Soldiers
People in the park

Aliens

Mom	Mom
Dad	Dad
Daughter	Jeebazz (JB)
Computer robot	Robo

Scene 1: In a spaceship flying through space near a funny planet

[The alien family is traveling through space. Their spaceship is like a car.]

JB *[Yawn]* Are we there Daddy? I'm bored.
Dad No, we aren't. It's a million light years to grandma's planet.
Mom Go to sleep for twenty years.
JB Sleep. I'm not tired! I'm bored! *[looks out of the window]* Hey Dad! What's that?
Dad It's a very small planet.
JB It's green and blue. It's pretty.
Robo It's called… Errrffff.
JB Errrffff?….. ruff *[starts laughing]* Are there lots of dogs there? Ruff Ruff Ruff!
Dad *[Laughing]* Ruff ruff.
JB Can we go and look at it? Please.
Mom No, we can't! It's dangerous.
Robo There aren't any intelligent creatures on Errrfff.
JB We can go and look.

[They all go to the window and start pointing. They think Earth looks very funny.]

Mom What are those strange things? There are lots of them.
Dad I think they're cars.
JB CARS! You're joking. They are boxes on wheels. But they're cute! Ha ha ha!

Scene 2: In the President's office

GP It's up there in the sky. Can you see it?
President Err… yes. What is it?
GP It isn't a plane. And it isn't a bird.
President No, it isn't a bird. What is it?
GP We don't know, sir. It's a UFO.
President A UFO! Aliens!??! ALIENS!!! Do something!
GP YES, SIR! Red alert! Every soldier in the country to central Park. NOW!!

Scene 3: In Central Park

[There are many soldiers lined up. The President, the General and the team are all standing and waiting. The reporter is talking to a camera.]

JJ This is Janey Jabber here on NBC News. We're bringing you a special report. I'm standing in Central Park, New York. In the sky I can see a large blue thing. It's a UFO. There are thousands of people here. We are all waiting to meet the aliens. Is this a friendly visit… or is it the end of the world? It's coming down! It's on the ground now… the doors are opening. The aliens are here!!

Mom Oh dear! They aren't very friendly.

Dad Maybe they're shy. Come on! Ruff ruff. *[laughing]*

JB They're wearing green uniforms.

Mom Yes, and they have horrible hats.

Dad I know! I can talk to them. *[clears his throat]*

JJ One alien is opening its mouth!

Dad TAKE ME TO YOUR LEADER.

[Dad, Mom and JB fall about laughing.]

Mom I know! WE COME IN PEACE.

[more giggling]

JB *[laughing]* Oh dad – this is brilliant!

GP They're attacking us!

Frank No, they aren't. They're talking to us!

Dad Oh dear. They don't like my jokes.

Frank Now they're laughing!

GP Soldiers! Get ready.

[soldiers step forward and look angry]

Scene 4: In Central Park

[The soldiers are lined up ready to fight the aliens. The aliens are still laughing. Frank pushes through the soldiers.]

Frank Hey! Wait a minute! They're friendly! *[walks forwards]* Hi! Who are you?

JB My name's Jeebazz.

Frank Cool! I'm Frank.

JB Who are *they*? They're boring!

Frank They're soldiers. They can't laugh. And that old man… he's the President. Anyway, where are you from?

JB Planet Giggle Five. We're on holiday. We're traveling to visit my grandmother.

Frank It's my holiday, too. Hey! Do you know E.T.?

JB It's my favorite movie!

Frank I love it too! *[shouts to the soldiers]* Hey, guys! Relax! They're cool!

JB Can you ride a bike?

Frank Of course I can. Come round and meet my mom and dad. They're cool too. You can ride my bike.

JB Brilliant!

[They wander off leaving the President and the soldiers looking confused.]

Verb list

be
become
buy
chat
check
cheer
choose
clean
come
come on
come out
complete
cook
count
cry
dance
dive
do
dribble
drink
earn
eat
fight
find
fish
fly
get dressed
get up
give
go
go back
go on
hang out
happen
hate
have
hear
help
hide
hurry up
identify
juggle
jump out

kid
kill
know
learn
leave
lie (on the beach)
like
listen
live
lock
look
look after
love
make
match
meet
need
play
put
read
repeat
rest
ride
run
sail
say
search for
see
shop
shout
sing
sit
skateboard
ski
sleep
smile
speak
stand
stop
stretch
sunbathe
surf
swim

take
take
take (it) off
take a photo
take out
talk
tell
text
think
tidy
touch
travel
try
turn
understand
use
visit
wake up
walk
want
wash
watch
wear
welcome
win
work
write

FORWARD!

Workbook

2

Starter

1 Write the missing letters.

1 A B C D *E*
2 F G H I ___
3 ___ L M N O
4 P Q R S ___
5 U V ___ X Y Z

2 Write the numbers.

8 *eight*
11 ______
22 ______
34 ______
13 ______
98 ______
70 ______
12 ______

3 Circle the correct result.

A 15 + 5 = *20*
fifty-five / twenty / twelve
B 9 + 18 = ______
twenty-four / twenty-six / twenty-seven
C 7 + 14 = ______
twenty-one / twenty-three / thirty
D 6 + 15 = ______
twenty-four / twenty / twenty-one
E 8 + 18 = ______
twenty-four / forty / twenty-six
F 10 + 20 = ______
sixty-four / thirty / fifty
G 14 + 40 = ______
fourteen / fifty-four / eighty-six
H 11 + 21 = ______
thirthy-two / ninety-one / seventy
I 58 + 18 = ______
sixty-seven / eighty-three / seventy-six

4 Write the names of the objects.

1 *book*
2 ______
3 ______
4 ______
5 ______
6 ______
7 ______
8 ______
9 ______

to be – affirmative singular

5 Write *am*, *is* or *are*.

1 I ______ from Brazil.
2 She ______ my sister.
3 Mark ______ from the USA.
4 He ______ my friend.
5 You ______ from London.
6 It ______ a notebook.
7 I ______ a student.

6 Write *'m*, *'s*, or *'re*.

I [1] *'m* a student. I [2] ________ from London. Mark [3] ________ a student. He [4] ________ from New York. Susan [5] ________ from Dallas. She [6] ________ twelve. You [7] ________ twelve. You [8] ________ in this class.

7 Write *this*, *that* , *these* or *those*.

1 *This* is my sister.

2 ________ is my book.

3 ________ is my shoe.

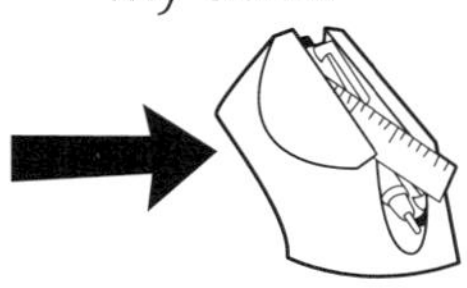

4 ________ is my pencil case.

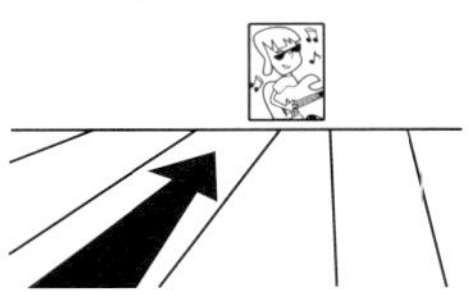

5 ________ is my poster.

6 ________ is my cat.

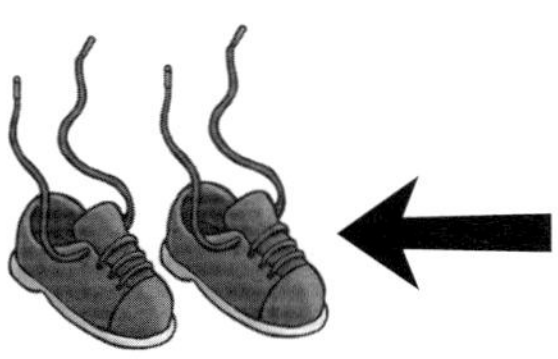

7 ________ are my shoes.

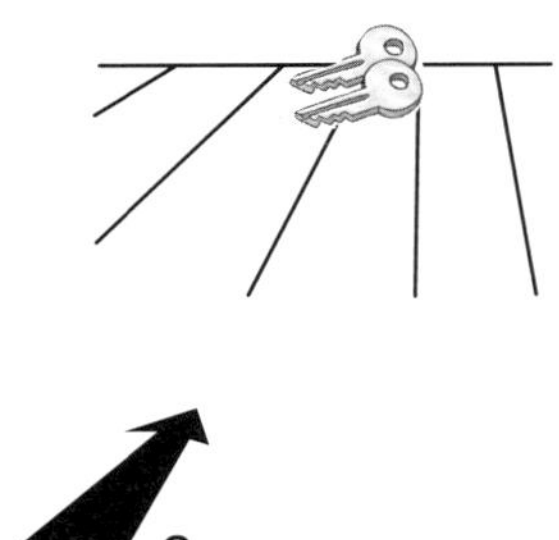

8 ________ are my keys.

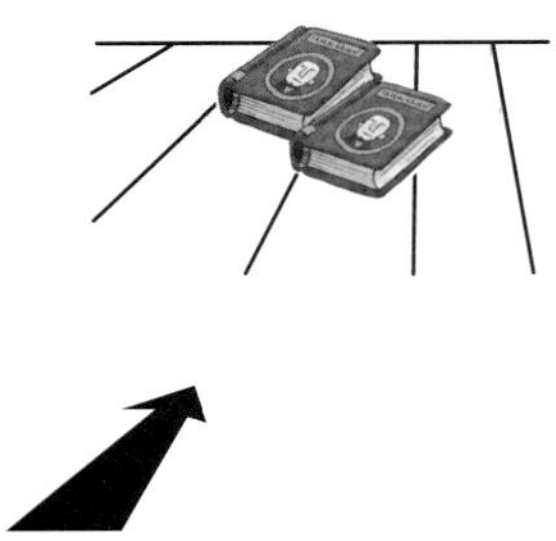

9 ________ are my books.

10 ________ is my teacher.

Subject pronouns

8 Complete the sentences with the subject pronouns in the box.

He It They I We Mary and Louise You She

1 *I* 'm twelve.
2 ________ 're my friend.
3 ________ 's from Britain.
4 ________ 's from New York. Her name is Sarah.
5 ________ 's a puppy!
6 ________ are new students. Our names are Tati and Jim.
7 ________ are 17 and 18.
8 ________ like black skirts.

Possessive adjectives

9 Complete the sentences with the correct possessive adjective.

1 This is ________ book. My name is on it.
2 ________ dog's name is Dug. She takes him for a walk every morning.
3 When ________ father is home, he doesn't make too much noise.
4 My mother told my brother and I to stay in ________ bedroom, because she had to finish cleaning the house. We share the bedroom because ________ house is not so big.
5 You have to do ________ homework before leaving.
6 The cat is eating ________ food.
7 Joanna and Dilbert love ________ son, Kevin. He's ________ only child.
8 When mom's not home, I have to take care of ________ sister.
9 Sandra likes ________ CDs, a lot! She organizes them in alphabetical order.
10 ________ mother called. She said you have to go to the supermarket with her.

1 Hi!

Presentation

1 Write the questions.

AR Excuse me. [1] *Are you Joe?*
Joe Yes.
AR Joe Murray?
Joe Yes, that's right.
AR Hi, Joe. [2] ________________? I'm Cynthia. [3] ________________?
Joe No, my bag is under my seat.
AR OK. Please come with me.
AR Wow, this is heavy! What's in here?
Joe Some of my favorite things: my skateboard, some books, magazines, a video game, an umbrella, my laptop, some snacks…
AR Wow… OK. So, [4] ________________, Joe?
Joe I'm from Pretoria.
AR Pretoria? [5] ________________?
Joe It's a city in South Africa.
AR South Africa… wow. Is this your first time in New York?
Joe Yes, it is.
AR Welcome to my hometown!
Joe Oh, a New Yorker! I'm a Yankees fan.
AR Yay, go Yankees! So… [6] ________________, Joe?
Joe I'm twelve. How old are you?
AR That's a secret!

2 Read the dialog again and complete.

1 The passenger's name is ____________.
2 There are many ________ in his bag.
3 Joe is from ________, a city in ________ ________.
4 This is Joe's ________ time in New York.
5 Joe Murray is ________ years old.

Vocabulary

3 Unscramble the letters and match the words to the pictures.

1 LAPEP = *apple*
2 KOBO = __________
3 NOLPLECHE = __________
4 POTPAL = __________
5 AZGIANME = __________
6 SAEORDABTK = __________
7 CSANK = __________
8 LARBELUM = __________
9 GOAEMDEIV = __________

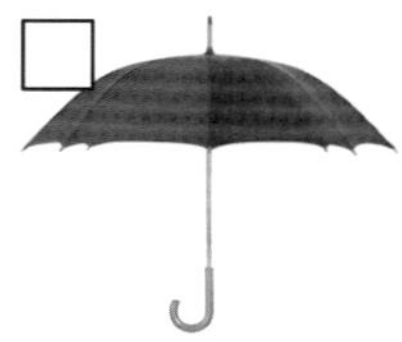

1

Language

Articles

1 Write *a*, *an* or *some*.

1 What's this? It's ___*a*___ book.
2 There are ________ students in the classroom.
3 It's ________ laptop.
4 It's ________ umbrella.
5 I have ________ new cell phone.
6 There are ________ magazines on the table.
7 It's ________ skateboard.
8 It's ________ delicious snack.
9 They have ________ old video games.
10 I eat ________ apple every day.

to be – questions

2 Circle the correct words.

1 Am / Is / Are you my friend?
2 Am / Is / Are I eleven?
3 Am / Is / Are she from Britain?
4 Am / Is / Are he a student?
5 Am / Is / Are it a computer?
6 Am / Is / Are I in this class?
7 Am / Is / Are you from London?
8 Am / Is / Are he a teacher?
9 Am / Is / Are she your mother?
10 Am / Is / Are you from New York?

3 Write the sentences as questions.

1 Vernon's twelve.
Is Vernon twelve?
2 Vicky's eleven.
____
3 He's a teacher.
____
4 She's a student.
____
5 It's a computer.
____
6 You're eleven.
____
7 I'm in this class.
____
8 It's a laptop.
____

4 Answer the quetions from exercise 3.

1 *Yes, he is*. (✔)
2 ________________________. (✘)
3 ________________________. (✘)
4 ________________________. (✔)
5 ________________________. (✔)
6 ________________________. (✘)
7 ________________________. (✔)
8 ________________________. (✘)

5 Correct the mistakes when necessary.

1 Is they home?
____
2 Are she alone?
____
3 Is your family big?
____
4 Are her parents nice?
____
5 Is Jonas and Jim related?
____
6 Is people nice?
____
7 Is the children at the party?
____

Language

Wh- questions

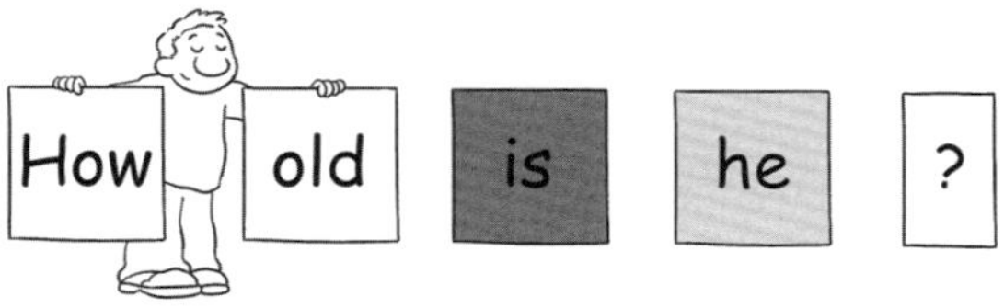

6 Write *wh-* questions. Use the correct form of the verb to be.

1 How old / you ?
How old are you?

2 What / your name ?
____

3 Where / he from ?
____

4 How old / I ?
____

5 Where / you from ?
____

6 What / the problem ?
____

7 Where / they from ?
____

8 How old / it ?
____

7 Read the profile and complete the paragraph.

Name: John Smith
Age: 12 years old
Hometown: Watertown
Favorite thing: swimming and dancing

Hi! My name *is John Smith* and I ____________ years old. I ____________ from ____________ and my favorite things ____________ and ____________.

8 Write a paragraph about this person.

Name: Brian Sapp
Age: 25 years old
Hometown: Venus
Favorite thing: observing humans

____
____
____
____
____
____

9 Create one character to write a paragraph about. Draw a picture of him/her, write its name, age, hometown and favorite thing. Be creative.

Name:
Age:
Hometown:
Favorite thing:

____
____
____
____
____
____

Communicate

1 Complete the conversation with the items a to h.

a Thank you
b K-I-E-R-O-N
c Good afternoon
d And where are you from
e Robertson
f Good morning
g What's your
h I'm fourteen

Student [1] *Good morning* ________
Receptionist Good morning?
Student Oh, sorry. Good afternoon.
Receptionist [2] ________. Are you a new student?
Student Yes, I am.
Receptionist [3] ________ first name?
Student Kieron.
Receptionist How do you spell that?
Student [4] ________
Receptionist [5] ________. What's your family name?
Student [6] ________.
Receptionist Robertson. OK. How old are you, Kieron?
Student [7] ________.
Receptionist [8] ________?
Student I'm from Manchester.
Receptionist OK. Thank you!

2 Name the objects.

1 
2 
3 
4 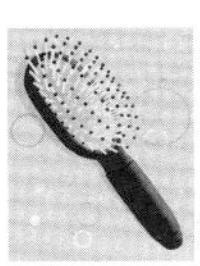
5 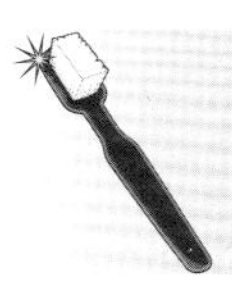
6 
7 
8 

3 Order this short conversation.

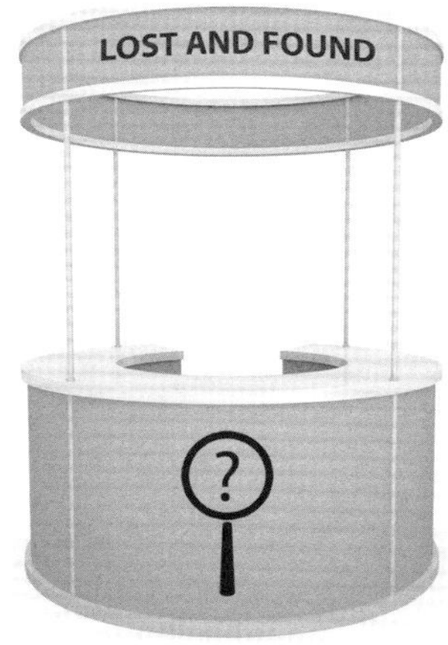

Oh! Thanks! ☐
Yes, I can't find my bag. ☐
What's in it? ☐
Hi, can I help you? *1*
There are some clothes, and my wallet. Oh, there's a key too. ☐
What color is it? ☐
It's black and white. ☐
OK, here's your bag! ☐

4 Now complete this conversation.

Clerk Hi, [1] *can I help you* ________?
Cynthia Yes, I can't find my wallet.
Clerk [2] ________?
Cynthia It's black.
Clerk [3] ________?
Cynthia There's some money, my ID card. Oh, there's my credit card too.
Clerk OK, [4] ________!
Cynthia Thank you!

5 Imagine you lost your school bag. Write a note describing it and what was inside.

Skills

This is my hometown, Pretoria. Look at how beautiful it is!

The National Zoological Gardens. That's a very [1]________ place, with lots of animals to see and play with.

This is the Freedom Park and it is [4]________! Just look at it!

These are The Union Buildings. The offices of the President are here. These are the most [2] ________ buildings in South Africa. Everyone who comes here visits them.

The Voortrekker monument really stands out in the city. It is big. No, it is more than big, it's [3] ________.

Reading

1 Complete the subtitles for the pictures with the adjectives from the box.

gigantic fun beautiful famous

2 Imagine your own city. Draw four items in it, like monuments, parks, stadiums, schools, and museums. Then, write sentences describing these places. Use some of the adjectives from the box.

beautiful cool nice fun gigantic famous tiny incredible

1 ________
____
____

2 ________
____
____

3 ________
____
____

4 ________
____
____

Look again

1 Find these words.

apple book cell phone laptop
magazine skateboard snack
umbrella video game

U	M	B	R	E	L	L	A	J	L	M	Q	S	B	T
Z	H	Q	J	R	C	Z	H	E	A	A	Y	R	U	L
E	F	Q	Q	M	L	L	G	V	P	D	P	K	K	Q
D	N	G	P	Z	T	B	Q	Z	P	O	C	T	G	Z
G	L	O	I	A	U	G	X	I	L	S	W	Y	O	U
Y	S	Y	H	D	R	A	O	B	E	T	A	K	S	P
K	E	N	S	P	Y	O	V	V	X	Z	X	N	X	D
H	M	E	R	C	L	K	O	O	B	E	A	S	I	H
J	A	Z	K	P	A	L	P	F	N	C	G	Y	H	A
R	G	V	Q	G	H	A	E	I	K	C	Z	G	X	D
Y	O	H	I	U	M	N	Z	C	K	H	E	F	N	A
E	E	W	O	S	O	A	N	P	Z	W	L	L	X	D
S	D	S	C	X	G	R	E	U	S	V	G	J	S	U
S	I	C	M	A	V	S	Z	I	G	D	A	L	H	A
S	V	U	M	F	I	Q	W	S	Z	N	V	H	F	J

2 Make affirmative sentences with *to be*.

1 I/from the USA
I am from the USA.

2 I/twelve
____

3 he/my teacher
____

4 she/my friend
____

5 he/from the USA
____

3 Make questions from the sentences in exercise 2.

1 *Where are you from?*
2 ________________
3 ________________
4 ________________
5 ________________

4 Complete the crossword.

Across

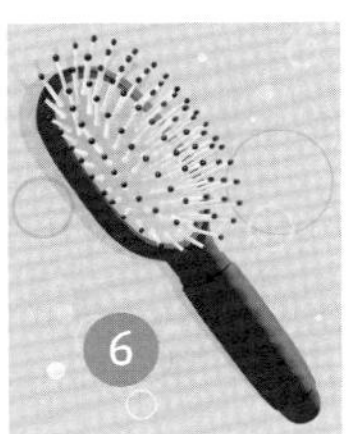

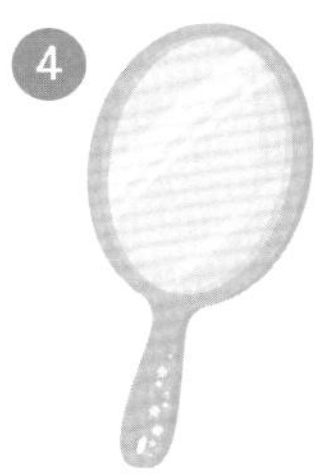

Down

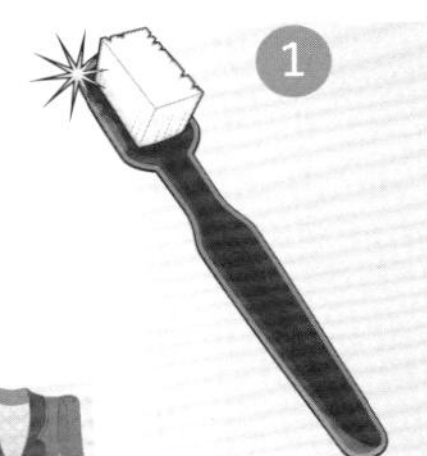

2 You can sleep in my room!

Vocabulary

1 Use the picture above to complete the puzzle. Write the names of the objects.

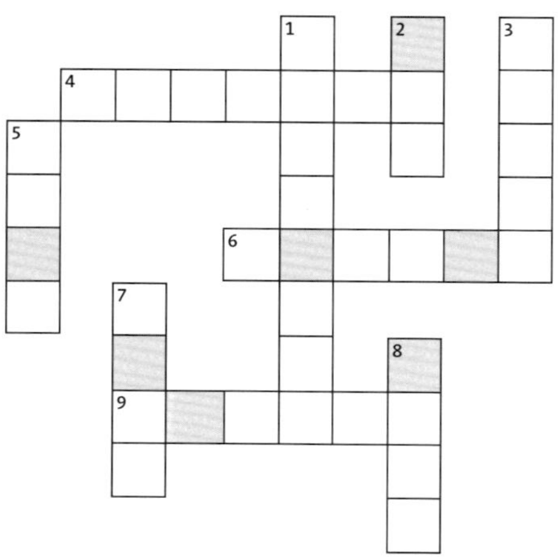

2 Use the shaded letters to make a word.

□□□□□□□

3 Use the picture above to complete the sentences. Look at letters a–g.

on	~~under~~	in	next to
in	behind	in front of	

Where is my homework?

a Is it *under* the table?
b Is it ________ the bed?
c Is it ________ the cupboard?
d Is it ________ of the lamp?
e Is it ________ the sofa?
f Is it ________ the football?
g Oh no! It's ________ my bag.

Language

There is/There are – affirmative

1 Write *there is* or *there are*.

1 *There are* shoes on the floor.
2 __________ a book next to the computer.
3 __________ a poster on the wall.
4 __________ an umbrella in the closet.
5 __________ two cats on the bed.
6 __________ three beds in the bedroom.
7 __________ a notebook on the chair.
8 __________ a cap under the bed.

There is/There are – negative

2 Write the negative form of the sentences in exercise 1.

1 *There aren't shoes on the floor.*
2 ____________________
3 ____________________
4 ____________________
5 ____________________
6 ____________________
7 ____________________
8 ____________________

There is / there are– questions

3 Write the sentences as questions.

1 There's a cat under your desk.
Is there a cat under your desk?
2 There are twenty-four students in your class.
____
3 There's an English book in your bag.
____
4 There are boys and girls in your class.
____
5 There's a computer on your desk.
____

4 Write the words in the correct order to make questions.

1 there / in / hand / your / pen / a / is ?
Is there a pen in your hand?
2 a / bag / chair / your / next / to / there / is ?
____
3 dogs / two / in / room / your / are / there ?
____
4 on / the / are / walls / there / posters ?
____

5 Answer the questions in exercise 3 about you.

1 ____________________
2 ____________________
3 ____________________
4 ____________________
5 ____________________

6 Write sentences about these items in your bag.

1 books
There are books in my bag.
There aren't any books in my bag.
2 umbrella
____
____
3 dog
____
____
4 pencils
____
____
5 board
____
____
6 T-shirt
____
____

Language

7 Look at the picture and check if the sentences are true or false. When they are false, correct them.

1 There are two toy cars on the desk.

____

2 There are three baseballs on the chair.

____

3 There aren't posters on the wall.

____

4 There are magazines on the floor.

____

5 There aren't CDs in his room.

____

Possessive *'s* – singular nouns

8 Write the possessive *'s* for each person.

1 That's *Pete's* brother, Sam. (Pete)
2 ________ grandfather is Scottish. (Claire)
3 Is this ________ mobile? (Martin)
4 ________ bike is cool! (Ellie)
5 Where is ________ house? (Joe)
6 ________ parents are vampires. (Vicky)

Possessive *s'* – plural nouns

9 Write *'s* or *s'*.

1 The boy*'s* clothes are on the floor.

2 The boy___ clothes are on the floor.

3 The actor___ book

4 The actor___ book

5 That's the dog___ bed.

6 That's the dog___ bed.

Communicate

1 Complete the chart.

Male	Female
father	1 ________
2 ________	wife
brother	3 ________
son	4 ________
grandson	5 ________
6 ________	aunt
7 ________	niece
cousin	8 ________
My mother and father are my 9 ________.	
The parents of my parents are my 10 ________.	

2 Look at the family tree. Complete the sentences with the correct information.

Douglas = Lily

Joanna = Luke — Jean = Patrick

Dylan, Sarah (children of Joanna = Luke) — Sophie, Rob, Adrian (children of Jean = Patrick)

1 Jean is Patrick's ________.
2 Joanna is Sophie's ________.
3 Douglas and Lily are Rob's ________.
4 Rob's ________ are Dylan and Sarah.
5 Douglas's ________ is called Luke.
6 Luke is Adrian's ________.
7 Dylan is Patrick's ________.
8 Joanna's ________ is called Luke.

3 Write the questions.

Dylan
Cousin
16
Tampa

You 1 *Is he your brother?*
Sophie No! He's my cousin!
You 2 ________
Sophie He's sixteen.
You 3 ________
Sophie He's name is Dylan.
You 4 ________
Sophie He's from Tampa.

4 Write and answer questions about Lily.

Lily
Grandmother
52
Albany

You ________ *mother?*
Sophie ________
You ________
Sophie ________
You ________
Sophie ________
You ________
Sophie ________

Skills

Punctuation

1 Complete the descriptions with the correct punctuation.

,	a comma
he's	an apostrophe
?	a question mark
.	a full stop
A	~~a capital letter~~

1 A~~(n)~~ ___*capital letter*___ begins a sentence.
2 A(n) ________________ ends a sentence.
3 A(n) ________________ breaks a sentence in the middle.
4 A(n) ________________ shows a question.
5 A(n) ________________ shows a contraction.

2 Rewrite the text with the correct punctuation.

im called will my grandmas called elizabeth shes the queen my brothers called harry hes twenty-three his favourite sports are rugby tennis and football

I'm ________________________________

____

____

____

____

____

Writing

3 Complete the information cards for the people in your family. Write the descriptions.

What is his/her name?
Is he/she your brother/aunt … ?
How old is he/she?
What is his/her favorite thing or sport?

Review

1 Complete the sentences with the correct word.

~~bedroom~~ dining room bathroom
living room hall kitchen

1 My *bedroom* is my favourite place.
2 There is a TV in the ________ .
3 The dog's bed is in the ________ .
4 Is there a table in your ________ ?
5 There isn't a cupboard in my ________ .
6 There are stairs and a lamp in the ________ .

2 Write the prepositions.

1 The bug is *behind* the box.
2 The bug is ________ the box.
3 The bug is ________ the box.
4 The bug is ________ the box.
5 The bug is ________ the box.
6 The bug is ________ the box.

3 Write questions with *there*.

1 lamp / next to / bed
Is there a lamp next to the bed?
2 chairs / dining room
____
3 poster / bathroom
____
4 three coats / hall
____
5 picture / dining room
____
6 pencils / on / desk
____

4 Write short answers to the questions in exercise 6.

1 (✔) *Yes, there is.*
2 (✔) ________
3 (✘) ________
4 (✘) ________
5 (✔) ________
6 (✘) ________

5 Complete the sentences.

1 My mother's son is my *brother* .
2 My dad's mother is my ________ .
3 My mum's brother is my ________ .
4 His son is my ________ .
5 My grandfather's ________ is my aunt.
6 My father's father is my ________ .
7 My mum's daughter is my ________ .
8 My brother's son is my ________ .

3 He has a beard

Presentation

1 Complete the conversation with the sentences from the box.

Look, I have long black hair and a green hat.
Oh, very funny, Joe.
Here! It's a monster!
And I'm Maid Marian!
~~Yes, we're ready!~~
Look at this horrible character!

Miss Brown OK! Do you have your costumes?

Ellie 1 *Yes, we're ready!* Who are you, May?

May I'm Robin Hood. 2 ________________.

Ellie It's a nice hat, but Robin Hood has a beard and he doesn't have glasses.

Mark And he's a man!

Miss Brown You're a very good Robin Hood, May.

Ellie 3 ________________

Mark No way Ellie! Maid Marian has straight, blond hair.

Ellie Well I'm Maid Marian with curly, blond hair. OK?

Joe Hey, Mark! 4 ________________ He has a really ugly face!

Mark Where?

Joe 5 ________________

Mark Really? My reflection in the mirror? 6 ________________

2 Look at the pictures and complete the descriptions.

1

My dad has _______ black _______ and brown eyes. He has a _______ but he doesn't have a _______ . He doesn't have _______ .

2

My grandmother has _______ white _______ and green eyes. She has _______ .

Language

Has – affirmative

1 Complete the sentences with *have* or *has*.

1 Simon *has* a gold tooth!
2 I _______ blond hair.
3 My daughters _______ glasses.
4 Jen and Pat _______ red hair.
5 He _______ a beard.
6 You _______ brown eyes.
7 She _______ green eyes.

Has – negative

2 Write negative sentences.

1 Amelia Spink has blue eyes.
Amelia Spink doesn't have blue eyes.
2 Mark and Ellie have glasses.
____
3 Your brothers have curly hair.
____
4 I have a scar on my hand.
____
5 Mr Andrews has long legs.
____
6 My brothers have big ears!
____

3 Write the words in the correct order to make negative sentences.

1 doesn't / Maid Marian / long / have / hair .
Maid Marian doesn't have long hair.
2 blond / My brother / doesn't / have / hair .
____
3 fur / my / dog / have / doesn't / pink .
____
4 family / have / ears / my / doesn't / big .
____
5 beard / have / Mrs Connor / a / doesn't .
____
6 you / ugly / don't / face / an / have .
____

4 Write *has* or *is* in the spaces.

This man's name [1]_______ John. He [2]_______ from Texas in the USA. John [3]_______ a really big hat on his head. He doesn't have hair under the hat – he [4]_______ bald! He [5]_______ big ears and he [6]_______ long, yellow teeth. He [7]_______ a long, black mustache. Under the mustache he [8]_______ a horrible scar. It isn't true! He isn't bald. He [9]_______ short black hair. Really, he [10]_______ a man called Doug. He [11]_______ an actor from Manchester. He [12]_______ in a film called The Man with the Scar!

5 Complete the sentences with two adjectives from the box.

long curly short big perfect white black green brown blond

1 She has _______ _______ hair.
2 He has _______ _______ teeth.
3 Dave has _______ _______ hair.
4 Tim has _______ _______ hair.
5 Lucy has _______ _______ eyes.

Language

Has – questions and short answers

6 Write the sentences as questions.

1 Robin Hood has a green hat.
Does Robin Hood have a green hat?

2 Maid Marian has a beard.
____

3 His parents have glasses.
____

4 Rex has a long tail.
____

5 They have long teeth.
____

6 He has a scar on his nose.
____

7 Her brothers have big ears.
____

8 Their cats have short brown fur.
____

7 Write the short answers to the questions in exercise 6.

1 (✔) *Yes, he does.*
2 (✘) ____________________
3 (✔) ____________________
4 (✔) ____________________
5 (✔) ____________________
6 (✘) ____________________
7 (✘) ____________________
8 (✘) ____________________

8 Write questions and answers for the people in the pictures.

Sophie

gold tooth
3 ____________________
____________________?
____________________ ✘

black hair
3 ____________________
____________________?
____________________ ✔

Jane and Kate

blond hair
5 ____________________?
____________________ ✔

glasses
6 ____________________?
____________________ ✘

Communicate

1 Rearrange the letters to make words.

1 HOSTR ☐☐☐☐☐
2 KWEA ☐☐☐☐
3 NEIC ☐☐☐☐
4 CENFINTDO ☐☐☐☐☐☐☐☐☐
5 DOL ☐☐☐
6 BULAEFUTI ☐☐☐☐☐☐☐☐☐
7 TAF ☐☐☐

2 Write the opposites of the words in exercise 1.

1 ______
2 ______
3 ______
4 ______
5 ______
6 ______
7 ______

3 Rearrange the letters in shaded boxes in exercise 1 to make a new word.

☐☐☐☐☐☐☐ Y

4 A girl is at the airport. She is looking for her cousin, Wayne. She is on the phone to her mom.

Mom Wayne has a brown bag.
Girl Three guys have brown bags!
[1] *Is Wayne short* ?
Mom No, he's tall.
Girl [2] ______ ?
Mom No, he has long hair.
Girl [3] ______ ?
Mom No, [4] ______ . He's young!
Girl [5] ______ glasses?
Mom No, [6] ______ .
Girl [7] ______ ?
Mom Yes, he has beautiful blue eyes.
Girl Oh yes! He's here! Wayne!

5 You are at the airport! Write a short conversation about this man.

You ______ ?
Mom ______ .
You ______ ?
Mom ______ .
You ______ ?
Mom ______ .
You ______ ?
Mom ______ .
You ______ ?
Mom ______ .
You ______ ?

Skills

Reading

1 Read the text. Complete the descriptions with the names.

Buzz Lightyear

Woody

Bo-peep

Mr. Potato Head

Well, he's not smart. He's funny and he's confident but he isn't smart! He is short. He has two eyes, a mouth and a nose, two ears and short legs. Sometimes his eyes and ears are in the wrong places! He's [1] ____________________.

OK, OK. What about me? I'm a funny guy. I'm not shy, I'm smart and brave. I have a long nose, short brown hair and a big hat. You know, I'm a cowboy! I'm [2] ____________________.

Her name's [3] ____________________.
She's beautiful. She has long blond hair and blue eyes under her big pink hat. She's young and she's shy.

I'm intelligent, I'm brave and I'm very confident, too. I have blue eyes and short hair and I'm very strong. Am I funny? What's funny? My name's [4] ____________________.

2 Answer the questions.

1 Who isn't very smart?

____

2 Who is smart and brave?

____

3 Who is intelligent, brave, strong and very confident?

____

4 Who is beautiful and shy?

____

Review

1 Write the words

1

______

2
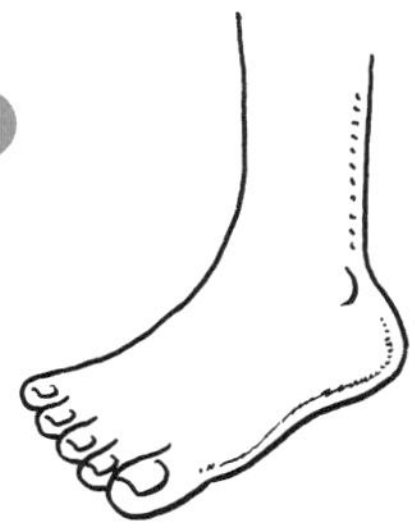
______

3

______

4
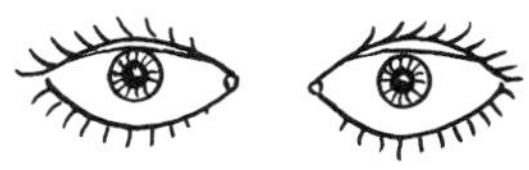
______

5

______

6

______

7
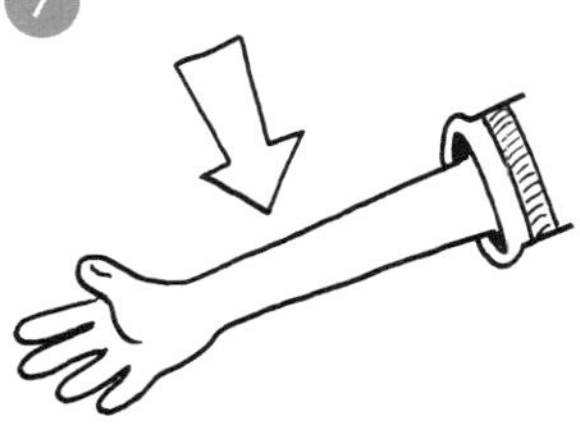
______

8

______

9

______

10

______

2 Complete the sentences with *have* or *has*.

1 I *have* long black hair.
2 My brother ________ a red pencil case.
3 Petra's dog ________ a long tail.
4 Robin and Marion ________ green hats.
5 She ________ blue eyes.
6 You ________ a new cell phone!
7 You and Gianluca ________ Italian names.

3 Make the sentences in exercise 2 negative.

1 *I don't have long black hair.*
2 ______
3 ______
4 ______
5 ______
6 ______
7 ______

4 Write the questions.

1 your grandparents / gray hair ?
Do your grandparents have gray hair?
2 Anna / blue eyes ?
______
3 she / long hair ?
______
4 your sister / brown eyes ?
______
5 your friends / bikes ?
______
6 they / gold teeth ?
______

4 She takes piano lessons with me

Presentation

1 **Complete the conversation with the sentences from the box.**

Does she go to your school? Do you smell that? ~~Who is that?~~ What's his name? But he doesn't play very well.

Mom [1]*Who is that?* ____________
Mark That's James. He sits next to me in English class.
Mom Who is this guy here? He looks nice.
Mark Kurt? Yeah, he is nice. We play basketball together sometimes. [2]____________
Mom And what about that boy?
Mark Oh, that's Ellie's boyfriend.
Mom Does Ellie have a boyfriend? [3]____________
Mark Nick. He takes the bus with me every morning.
Mom I see. And what about this cute girl?
Mark Who – Natalie?
Mom Yeah. [5]____________
Mark Yes, she does. She takes piano lessons with me on Thursdays. She's really nice. She knows judo! And she speaks fluent French! And she –
Mom Hmm... [6]____________
Mark Smell what?
Mom The smell of romance in the air!
Mark Mom!!!

2 **Rearrange the letters to make the names of activities.**

1 THWCA VT ☐☐☐☐☐ ☐☐
2 PAYL CECROS ☐☐☐☐ ☐☐☐☐☐☐
3 TEG PU ☐☐☐ ☐☐
4 GO OT DBE ☐☐ ☐☐ ☐☐☐
5 AHEV BKTEFAASR ☐☐☐☐ ☐☐☐☐☐☐☐☐☐
6 HAEV RDNENI ☐☐☐☐ ☐☐☐☐☐☐
7 TIVSI MY FNDIRE ☐☐☐☐☐ ☐☐ ☐☐☐☐☐☐
8 KATE A WERHSO ☐☐☐☐ ☐ ☐☐☐☐☐☐
9 TEG RSDEDSE ☐☐☐ ☐☐☐☐☐☐☐

Language

Simple present – affirmative

1 Complete the text. Use the correct form of the verbs from the box.

cook	get dressed	get up	go
meet	talk	walk	watch	~~work~~

I'm forty-five years old and I [1] _work_ in a school. I [2] ______ at seven o'clock, I [3] ______ and I [4] ______ to school. I [5] ______ a lot of people. In the evening I [6] ______ home and I [7] ______ dinner for my family. We [8] ______ TV and we [9] ______ about the day. What do I do? I'm the head teacher!

2 Complete the sentences about my sister and me. Write the verbs in the correct form.

1 I have breakfast at seven. My sister _has_ breakfast at eight.
2 I go to school by bike. She ______ to school by bus.
3 I study at home. She ______ on the bus.
4 I do my homework in my room. She ______ her homework in the kitchen.
5 I play the piano. She ______ the guitar.
6 I watch TV. She ______ DVDs.
7 I go to sleep at ten. She ______ to sleep at eleven.

Simple present – negative

3 Circle the correct words.

1 Pablo don't / (doesn't) do his homework.
2 I don't / doesn't have lunch at school.
3 Miss Troy don't / doesn't play soccer.
4 The men don't / doesn't visit Mr. Murray.
5 Giraffes don't / doesn't eat peanuts.
6 Joe don't / doesn't talk about his dad.

4 Put the words in the correct order.

1 at / six o'clock / get up / I don't .
______
2 ride / Mark / his bike / doesn't / to school .
______
3 to work / doesn't / go / May's mom .
______
4 don't / Mark and Ellie / Spanish / speak .
______
5 doesn't / Joe / the men / speak to .
______

5 Write negative sentences.

1 My grandparents live in London.
My grandparents don't live in London.
2 Michelle works here.
______
3 Mark juggles with eggs!
______
4 My brother rides his bike to school.
______
5 We have guitar lessons.
______
6 They speak Spanish.
______

Language

Simple present – questions and short answers

6 **Complete the questions and answers with *do, does, don't* or *doesn't*.**

1 _Does_ Michael meet his friends?
Yes, he _does_ .

2 _______ Michael become invisible?
No, he _______ .

3 _______ the men talk to Joe's dad?
No, they _______ .

4 _______ Joe's dad work at home?
Yes, he _______ .

5 _______ Ellie's parents work in a café?
Yes, they _______ .

7 **Write the questions. Then answer the questions about you.**

1 get up at nine o'clock?
Do you get up at nine o'clock ?
Yes, I do. / No, I don't .

2 go to school by bus?
_______________________________ ?
_______________________________ .

3 watch TV before school?
_______________________________ ?
_______________________________ .

4 do your homework in the kitchen?
_______________________________ ?
_______________________________ .

5 go to bed at midnight on Saturday?
_______________________________ ?
_______________________________ .

8 **Complete the story with the verbs from the box. Write the verbs in the correct form.**

cook get ~~get up~~ have sing visit not sing talk not talk ride not walk

The Happy Postman

The Happy Postman [1] _gets up_ at five and he [2]_______ dressed. He [3]_______ bacon and eggs for breakfast at six then he [4]_______ his bike to work. He's happy! He [5]_______ lots of houses and he [6]_______ to lots of people. He's a friendly postman, too! He [7]_______ lunch at eleven. He [8]_______ , because he's the Happy Postman!

BUT, after lunch he isn't happy. He [9]_______ because he isn't happy. He [10]_______ to people because he isn't friendly. He [11]_______ , he *runs*!
Why? Because he's scared! He's scared of Superdog!

Communicate

1 **What time is it? Write the times.**

1

It's ten o'clock .

2
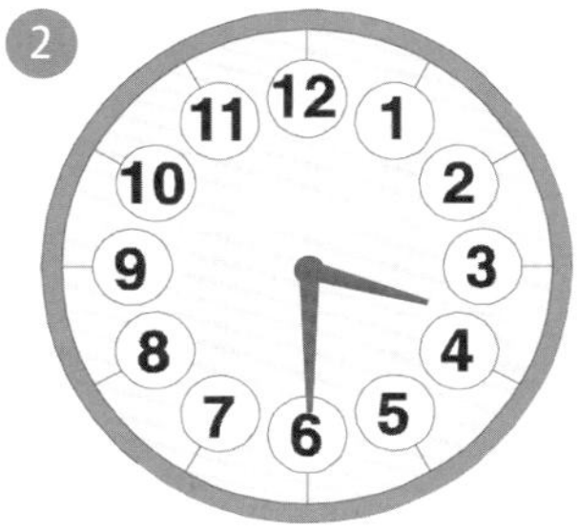

______

3

______

4
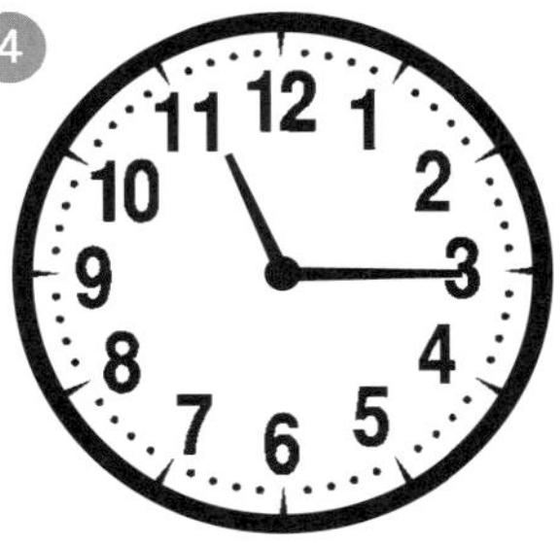

______

5

______

6

______

2 **Write the days of the week.**

1 mnadoy ______
2 tsuadey ______
3 wasedendy ______
4 tdrshauy ______
5 fiadry ______
6 staduary ______
7 sdnauy ______

3 **Write Mark's questions about times.**

1 get up?
What time do you get up? ?
2 get dressed?
______?
3 go to school?
______?
4 have dinner?
______?
5 go to bed?
______?

All about you

4 **Answer Mark's questions in exercise 3 about you.**

1 ______
2 ______
3 ______
4 ______
5 ______

Skills

me – wet and cold in the rain

Hi Mom and Dad,

How are you? I'm OK but it's cold and wet here at Cold Camp.

We get up at six thirty and take a shower. The water's cold! Then we get dressed and clean our rooms. After that, at seven o'clock, we have breakfast. We can choose water or orange juice to drink and have old bread to eat. Yuk!

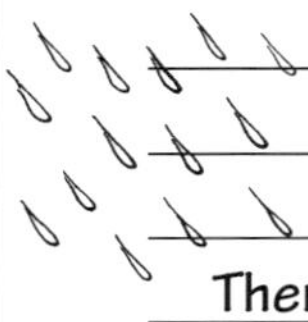

In the morning we do activities. We learn a new activity every day. Lunch is at twelve thirty. We have cold pizza. Then we go outside in the rain. Why? Because they lock the doors! They give us a map and we go for a walk. A wet walk. Then we swim in the cold river!

There isn't a TV here. In the evening we talk. It's OK and I have two friends. We play cards and tell stories. I go to bed at nine o'clock because it's cold!

I don't like this camp. I want to go home and I want to go to school!

Jake XX

Reading

1 Put these activities in the order of the text. Number them 1 to 10.

- a get dressed ☐
- b go to bed ☐
- c swim ☐
- d get up *1*
- e have breakfast ☐
- f clean the room ☐
- g play cards ☐
- h learn a new activity ☐
- i go for a walk ☐
- j take a shower ☐

2 Read the text. Are these sentences true or false?

1 *false* Jake is happy at Cold Camp.
2 _____ He takes a shower with cold water.
3 _____ For breakfast he has bacon and eggs.
4 _____ At twelve thirty he goes for a walk.
5 _____ In the evening he watches TV.
6 _____ He goes to bed at ten o'clock.
7 _____ He has two friends at the camp.
8 _____ He wants to go to school!

Writing

3 Write a letter about a day at the camp. You can use Jake's letter to help you.

Who is the letter to?
Hi __________ .
How are you? I'm fine/OK.

Describe your morning routine
get up / get dressed
have a shower or a wash
have breakfast (what do you eat?)
I get up at _______ Then _______
After that __________

Describe your afternoon routine
have lunch / do _______ /
play _______
At twelve thirty I __________

What do you do in the evening?
do my homework / watch TV /
play _____ / visit _____

Finish your description
And that's a day at the camp!

Finish the letter
All the best / See you / _______

Review

1 Put the words in the correct box.

a movie   a shower   computer games
friends   my grandmother   the piano
to bed   ~~to school~~   ~~TV~~

go	
to school	______

play	
______	______

visit	
______	______

watch	
TV	______

take
______

2 Write sentences using the simple present.

1 he / get up / at five o'clock
He gets up at five o'clock.
2 she / ride / her bike to school
______
3 we / go / to sleep at nine o'clock
______
4 they / walk / to school
______
5 she / study / in the dining room
______
6 he / visit / his aunt on Saturdays
______

3 Complete the text. Write the verbs in the correct form.

I [1]______ (get up) at seven o'clock. My dad [2]______ (get up) at 3:30! He [3]______ (work) in a factory. He [4]______ (walk) to work. Me and my brother [5]______ (ride) our bikes to school. [6]______ (he help) me with my homework? No, he [7]______ (not do)! What time [8]______ (we go) to bed? Well, he [9]______ (go) to bed at 8:30!

4 Write the time in words.

1  *It's five fifteen.*

2  ______

3 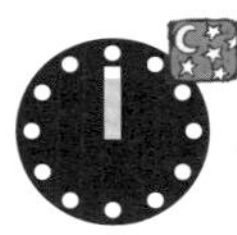 ______

4  ______

5 Complete the conversations.

1 A *What* time *do* you get up?
B I ______ ______ at ______.
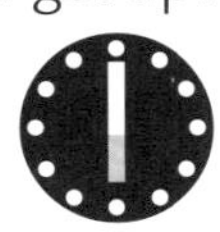

2 A ______ you ______ to bed at ten o'clock?
B No, I ______. I ______ to bed at ______.

5 What are you watching?

Presentation

1 **Put the cards in the correct order to make the dialogue. Write the order here.**

1 *E* 2 ☐ 3 ☐ 4 ☐ 5 ☐

A

Ellie What?
Mark I'm just kidding!

B

Mark What are you doing?
Ellie I'm dribbling the ball, like a soccer player.
Mark You're dancing like you have two left feet.

C

Mark The USA are playing against Brazil.
Ellie Cool! What's the score?
Mark Brazil is winning, of course. Five to one.
Ellie Five to one? You're kidding! That's horrible.
Mark No it's not. I'm cheering for Brazil!

D

Ellie Why?
Mark The Brazilian team has talent.
Ellie No, Brazil has Neymar! Anyway, Americans have talent too! See?

E

Ellie What are you watching, Mark?
Mark I'm watching a soccer game.
Ellie Who's playing?

2 **Read the descriptions. What jobs do the people do?**

1. *I start work at seven thirty but I often work at night. I work inside and I wear a uniform. I help the doctors and I work with people. They are usually in bed. What's my job?*
I'm a __________________ .

2. *I start my day at nine forty-five. Usually I work inside but sometimes I work outside. I work with people, with books and computers. I'm twelve and I don't earn money, of course!*
I'm a __________________ !

3. *I'm a man but my wife does the same job. I get up at five o'clock! I usually work outside. I work with animals and machines. I don't wear a uniform and I don't earn lots of money. What am I?*
I'm a __________________ .

3 **Choose a job and write about it.**

What time do you start/finish?
Do you wear a uniform?
Do you work usually inside or outside?
Do you work with people, animals, computers, ...?
Do you earn a lot of money?

____
____
____
____
____
____
____

Language

1 Read the screen. Then answer the questions.

Alice: How are you, Jessie?
Jessie: I'm feeling OK but I can't go outside. Grrr!
Alice: What are you doing?
Jessie: I'm sitting with Jack. We're watching our friends. They're playing in the garden.

2 users
Alice
Jessie

1 Who is Jessie writing to? *Alice*
2 Who is sitting with Jessie? ________
3 Who are they watching?
____
4 Where are the kids playing?
____

2 Complete Jessie's webchat. Write the verbs in the correct form.

Alice Oh. What are they doing?
Jessie They [1]*are having* (have) a good time. Liz and Max [2]________ (play) soccer. Lucy and Jake [3]________ (juggle). They're good!
Alice Are Mark and Bex there?
Jessie Mark [4]________ (watch) Liz and Max. He [5]________ (laugh)! Bex [6]________ (read) a magazine.
Alice Where's Dan?
Jessie He's at home. He [7]________ (look after) the baby.
Alice And Tony?
Jessie Tony [8]________ (talk).
Alice Who's he talking to?
Jessie Katie. I think he likes her!

3 Read Jessie's webchat in exercise 2 and write the names on the picture below.

Language

4 Complete the conversation. Write sentences in the present continuous.

1 **Spike** what / you do / Mary ?
What are you doing Mary?

2 **Mary** I / watch / two men .

3 **Mary** they / go / into Pat's house .

4 **Mary** they / come out !

5 **Mary** they / carry a TV !

6 **Spike** what / you do / now ?

7 **Mary** I / call the police.

8 **Spike** what / the men / do now ?

9 **Mary** they / walk to their car .

10 **Mary** the police / arrive !

11 **Mary** they / shout / at the men !

12 **Spike** what / happen now ?

13 **Mary** the men / sit / in the police car .

14 **Mary** the police officers / smile .

5 Correct these statements.

1 The men are carrying a fridge.
No they aren't. They're carrying a TV.

2 Mary is calling her friends.

3 The men are running to their car.

4 The men are smiling.

Communicate

1 **Complete the puzzle.**

2 **Complete these phone phrases.**

1 ___*How*___ are you?
2 I'm ________ , thanks.
3 Oops. I can't ________ ________ !
4 ________ ________ calling.
5 See ________ ________ .

3 **Complete the phone conversation between Peter and Eddie. Use the items from the box.**

are you	are you	Bye	Eddie
~~Hello~~	thanks	you play	you soon

Peter [1] ___*Hello*___ ?
Eddie Peter? It's [2] ________ .
How [3] ________ ?
Peter I'm fine, [4] ________ . Hey, I'm playing volleyball with Mark and Jen. Can [5] ________ ?
Eddie Yes, I can play. Where [6] ________ ?
Peter At school.
Eddie Great! See [7] ________ .
Peter [8] ________ .

Skills

Hi Pat,

I'm visiting my Uncle Robert's school in Cape Town today. He's a teacher and I'm in his class. His students are asking me about Manchester. They are really friendly. At the moment the students in Uncle Robert's class are writing about Manchester and I'm waiting for lunch. They're wearing shorts and trainers – it's very hot here today. I don't usually wear skirts but right now I don't like wearing my jeans! Outside, the sun's shining. A class is sitting outside. They're all studying – actually I think one of the boys is sleeping! There! The bell is ringing and it's time for lunch. The boy outside is looking for his friends but they're running to lunch!

Please write to me!

All the best,

Fiona x

Reading

1 Read the text. Circle the correct words.

1 Pat / Fiona / Robert is writing a letter.
2 Robert is a headmaster / student / teacher.
3 Fiona's from Manchester / Cape Town / Italy.
4 At the moment the students are asking questions / sleeping / writing.
5 Fiona's wearing a skirt / shorts / jeans.

Writing

2 It's night time and you can't sleep. Write to your friend. Talk about what you can see and hear in your house or outside.

Start your letter

Hi Pete,

What time is it?

It's ________ .

Can you hear a person or animal? Where are they? What are they doing?

brother / sister / dog / cat

He's / She's / It's …

Describe your situation

Where are you?

bedroom / kitchen / living room

What are you doing?

writing / listening to music

Finish your letter

Please write to me! / All the best,

Review

1 Complete the sentences in the Present continuous.

do lie play ~~read~~ sit walk watch wear

1 I *am reading* a book about cats. (✔)
2 We ________ a funny film. (✔)
3 He ________ soccer. (✔)
4 She ________ her new boots. (✘)
5 They ________ to school. (✘)
6 You ________ in my chair! (✔)
7 I ________ my homework. (✘)
8 We ________ on the beach. (✘)

2 Write questions.

1 (your sister / laugh)
A: *Is your sister laughing?*
B: Yes, she is.
(what / she / laugh at)
A: ________________
B: A show on TV.

2 (Jenny / watch TV)
A: ________________
B: Yes, she is.
(what / she / watch on TV)
A: ________________
B: She's watching soccer.

3 (they / running to school)
A: ________________
B: Yes, they are.
(why / they / run to school)
A: ________________
B: Because they are late.

3 Write affirmative sentences (✔), negative sentences (✘) or questions (?). Write the verbs in the correct form.

1 I / lie / on the beach ✔
I am lying on the beach.
2 some boys / skateboard / near us ✔
____
3 my sister / shop ✘
____
4 what / you / do ?
____
5 who / they / talk to ?
____
6 you / hang out / with Tony ?
____
7 my parents / swim / at the moment ✘
____
8 my dad / surf ✔
____
9 my mom and my brother / sunbathe ✘
____
10 we / eat / ice cream ✔
____

4 Complete the phone conversation.

1 Hello Maria, *it's* Pablo.
2 ________ Pablo!
3 Hi! ________ are ________ ?
4 What ________ you ________ at the moment?
5 I ________ talk now!
6 I'm ________ my mom's phone.
7 OK. ________ ________ later.
8 Thanks for ________ .

6 Can you juggle?

Presentation

1 Complete the conversation with the phrases from the box.

Why? Can you juggle? Are you hungry, Joe? Be careful, Mark! Not bad. Can you cook, Joe?

Mark Hey Joe! [1]<u>*Can you juggle?*</u>
Joe No, I can't. Can you?
Mark Yes, I can. It's easy… two tomatoes….
Grandma That's easy! Even *I* can do that! Watch…
Ellie Wow! Even Grandma can juggle!
Grandma Not bad, eh?
Mark Yes, but two tomatoes and an onion?
Joe Wow! [2]____________ Hey, you *can* juggle!
Mark … and two eggs…
Ellie [3]____________
Mark And another egg. Oops!
Ellie Urgh!!
Mark [4]____________
Joe Actually, yes I am. [5]____________
Mark Because there's an omelet – on the floor!
Grandma [6]____________
Joe No, but I can make hamburgers. Hamburgers, guys?

Vocabulary

2 Rearrange the letters to make words.

1 KOCO ☐☐☐☐
2 NRU ☐☐☐
3 GGJLEU ☐☐☐☐☐☐
4 EDIR ☐☐☐☐
5 ESU ☐☐☐
6 WSMI ☐☐☐☐
7 APYL ☐☐☐☐

Language

can – affirmative

1 Complete the sentences with *can* and the verbs from the box.

use	swim	play	speak	lift	run

1 My teacher *can* *speak* French and English.
2 I ________ ________ the piano.
3 My mom ________ ________ a computer.
4 My dog ________ ________ underwater!
5 Jack Parr ________ ________ 1 ton.
6 Dash ________ ________ through walls.

can – negative

2 Write negative sentences.

1 Joe can juggle.
Joe can't juggle.
2 Helen Parr can fly.
____
3 Pablo can ride a horse.
____
4 I can cook a pizza.
____
5 My brother can play soccer.
____
6 My grandfather can use a cell phone.
____

3 Complete the sentences. Use *can* or *can't*.

1 

My teacher *can speak* Chinese.

2 
Jo ________________.

3 
My grandfather ________________.

4 
I ________________.

5 
My dad ________________.

6 
Francesca ________________.

7 
She ________________.

8 

They ________________.

Language

can – questions and short answers

4 Write the questions and short answers.

1 Joe can juggle. ✘
Can Joe juggle ______?
No, he can't ______.

2 Ellie can ride a bike. ✔
______?
______.

3 Helen Parr can stretch her body. ✔
______?
______.

4 Violet can run through walls. ✘
______?
______.

5 My friends and I can fly. ✘
______?
______.

6 Your teacher can speak Chinese. ✘
______?
______.

7 Violet can make a force field. ✔
______?
______.

8 You can do this exercise! ✔
______?
______.

5 Write the conversation with Dan about his family. Use the chart to answer the questions.

	Dan	Kate	Mom	Dad
Speak Italian	✘	✘	✔	✘
Play the guitar	✔	✘	✘	✔
Cook omelets	✘	✘	✔	✔
Ride a horse	✘	✘	✔	✘
Use a computer	✔	✘	✔	✔

1 **You** you / the guitar ?
Can you play the guitar?
Dan *Yes, I can.*

2 **You** your dad / speak Italian ?
______
Dan ______

3 **You** your parents / use a computer ?
______
Dan ______

4 **You** your mom / ride a horse ?
______
Dan ______

5 **You** your dad / cook omelets ?
______
Dan ______

6 **You** Kate / play the guitar ?
______
Dan ______

7 **You** Kate / use a computer ?
______
Dan ______
Kate's only two!

Communicate

1 Complete the puzzle.

Across

3
7
8
9
13
15
16
17

Down

1
2
4
5
6
7
10
11
12
13
14

2 Complete the conversation between the waiter and the customer.

Skills

and and *but*

1 Combine these sentences with *and* and *but*.

1 Jess can juggle. She can cook an omelete. She can't skateboard.
Jess can juggle and she can cook an omelete but she can't skateboard.

2 I can play the guitar. I can't play the piano. I can't sing.

3 Renne can speak English. She can speak French. She can speak Swahili.

4 Matt can speak English. He can't speak Italian.

5 I can ride a horse. I can ride a bike. I can't skateboard.

2 Write sentences about you and the following activities.

1 soccer/volleyball

2 swim/dance

3 cook/do the dishes

4 run/jump

5 play the piano/play hide and seek

Writing

3 Write a letter about you. Use Ella's letter as a model.

Hello,

My name's Ella Rose. I'm thirteen years old. I am from California. I can play the guitar and the violin but I can't play the piano. I can sing and dance but I can't ride a horse.

Bye,
Ella

Review

1 Write the correct verbs to complete the phrases.

1 *use* ___________ a computer
2 ___________ in the river
3 ___________ baseball
4 ___________ a bike
5 ___________ a pizza
6 ___________ Italian
7 ___________ two kilometers
8 ___________ a horse
9 ___________ the piano

2 Write affirmative sentences with *can*.

become fly play play ride run speak

1 Superman / very fast
Superman can fly very fast.
2 Viggo Mortensen / Italian, Spanish and English
____
3 Harry Potter / invisible
____
4 Neymar / soccer
____
5 Jamie Foxx / the piano
____
6 Ewan McGregor / motorcycle
____
7 Will Ferrell / a marathon (forty-two kilometers)
____

3 Complete the sentences with *can't*.

become carry cook make play run swim use

1 She *can't play* an instrument.
2 English people ___________ pasta!
3 Dogs ___________ underwater.
4 Harry Potter ___________ through walls.
5 Spiderman ___________ invisible
6 Batman ___________ a force field.
7 I ___________ one ton.
8 My grandmother ___________ a cell phone.

4 Put the questions in order.

1 Can / friend / Russian? / speak / your
Can your friend speak Russian?
2 Can / invisible? / become / you
____
3 your / Can / teacher / a / use / computer?
____
4 Marco / play / and Gaia / Can / tennis?
____
5 the / you / play / Can / violin?
____
6 they / an / cook / omelet? / Can
____
7 horse? / a / ride / you / Can
____
8 Lucie / three / Can / juggle / apples?
____

5 Write the names of the items.

1 
orange juice

2 
____

3 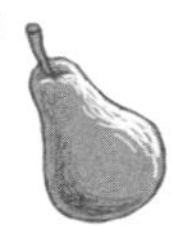
____

4 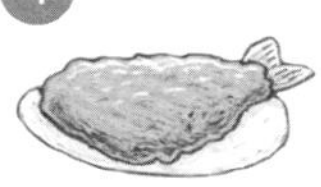
____

5 
____

6 
____

7 
____

8 
____

9 
____

7 Look at that giraffe!

Presentation

1 Complete the conversation with the phrases from the box.

He doesn't have hands! Are you kidding? How do you know it's a "he?" Look at that giraffe! do you have food for the giraffe?

Ellie	Wow! [1] *Look at that giraffe!* If you call it, it comes to you.
Mark	Here, giraffe! Here, boy!
Joe	It's not a dog, Mark. It wants food.
Ellie	Give it peanuts.
Joe	Peanuts? [2] ________________ Come on – it's not an elephant!
Ellie	Mrs. Murray, [3] ________________
Mrs Murray	We can get giraffe food at the store there.
Joe	Thanks, Mom. Here… see?
Ellie	Cool.
Joe	If you give him food, he stays. He loves it.
Mark	[4] ________________
Joe	It's a he. His name is Mark.
Ellie	Ha ha!
Mark	Hey! If he wants to drink, I have some water here!
Ellie	Don't be silly! [5] ________________
Mark	Oh yeah.

Vocabulary

2 Match the correct words together.

1 A snake's home is	a on a farm.
2 A dog's home is	b very clever animals.
3 A cow's home is	c my pet.
4 An elephant is	d in a house.
5 A goldfish's home is	e in the wild.
6 This rabbit is	f a really big animal.
7 Monkeys are	g in water.
8 A horse's home is	h on a farm.

Language

Countable and uncountable nouns

1 Are these words countable or uncountable? Write C or U.

1 potato ______
2 pasta ______
3 pea ______
4 bean ______
5 orange juice ______
6 salt ______
7 omelet ______
8 tomato ______
9 egg ______
10 hot chocolate ______

2 Write the correct form of the nouns.

1 There's some *lemonade* here. (lemonade)
2 There are some ____________ in the kitchen. (apple)
3 I have some ____________. (egg)
4 Julie has some ____________. (water)
5 There's some ____________ in the fridge. (milk)
6 Peter has some ____________. (pear)
7 I have some ____________. (French fries)
8 Can I have some ____________ in my coffee? (sugar)

3 Circle the correct words.

1 I have (a) / some sandwich.
2 She has a / some sugar.
3 There's a / some water here.
4 I have a / some banana.
5 I can see a / some lemonade.
6 There's a / some burger in the house.
7 You have a / some eggs.
8 I have a / some apples.

some – affirmative and *any* – negative and questions

4 Complete the conversation. Write *some* or *any*.

Pat Do you have [1] *some* water?
Sue I have [2] __________ water, but I don't have [3] __________ milk.
Pat Is there [4] __________ milk in the kitchen?
Sue No, there isn't [5] __________ milk in the house.
Pat Do you have [6] __________ sugar?
Sue Sorry, I don't have [7] __________ sugar. There's [8] __________ salt here.
Pat How about eggs? Do we have [9] __________ eggs?
Sue No. We don't have [10] __________ eggs.
Pat OK. We have [11] __________ water and [12] __________ salt but we don't have [13] __________ milk, sugar or eggs. Breakfast is very boring today!

5 Look at the picture and complete the sentences.

There is some milk.
There isn't __________ sugar.
There isn't any __________.
There is __________ orange juice.
There are some __________.

Language

6 Write *how much* or *how many*.

1 *How many* people are here?
2 __________ eggs do we have?
3 __________ lemonade is there?
4 __________ orange juice do we have?
5 __________ apples are there?
6 __________ sugar is there?
7 __________ milk is there?
8 __________ bananas do we have?
9 __________ water is there?
10 __________ friends do we have?

"Zero" conditional – affirmative

7 Match a cause to an effect.

1 If you want to watch the movie, ...
2 If there is a software problem, ...
3 If they call you on the phone, ...
4 If the traffic light is red, ...
5 If I go to this restaurant, ...
6 If you want to have good grades, ...
7 If you travel ...
8 If you don't brush your teeth ...
9 If you eat too much chocolate, ...
10 If it rains, ...

[*5*] I always order the same thing.
[ ] study more!
[ ] the computer stops.
[ ] turn on the TV now.
[ ] you have to stop your car.
[ ] don't answer.
[ ] I have to turn my computer off.
[ ] your breath smells really bad!
[ ] bring me a souvenir.
[ ] you get pimples.

"Zero" conditional + imperative

8 Complete the sentences below with words from the box.

are (2x)	want (2x)	give	know

1 If you *know* the answer, don't say anything.
2 If you ________ tired, go home.
3 If I ________ you an order, obey.
4 If you ________ to ask a question, raise your hand.
5 If you ________ in the English class, don't speak Portuguese.
6 If you ________ to use the cell phone, leave the class.

9 Write some of your house rules about these situations.

1 bad grades
If I get bad grades, I...
2 not arriving home on time
____
3 not doing the homework
____
4 video games
____
5 playing outside
____
6 going out at night
____
7 cleaning the bedroom
____
8 doing the dishes
____
9 inviting people to go to your house
____
10 fighting with siblings
____

Communicate

1 Look at the signs and complete the conversation accordingly.

1

2

3

4

5

6

7

8

Jimmy: Excuse me, how do I get to the school?

Ann: The school? [1]__________, it is a little complicated. First, [2]__________ for 2 blocks on this street. [3]__________ before the yellow supermarket, OK? [4]__________ before the red supermarket. [5]__________ on the avenue for 3 blocks and [6]__________ after the bank. [7]__________ after the bank. The school is on your right, next to the park.

2 Follow the instructions. Which animal can you see?

1 Turn left. Then turn right.
elephant

2 Go straight. Turn right. Go straight. Turn left.
____

3 Go straight. Turn left. Turn right. Turn left.
____

3 Write the directions to see these animals.

1 monkey
____
____

2 snake
____
____

3 giraffe
____
____

Skills

My favorite animal

My favorite animal is my friend's cat, Maurice. My friend is called Rose. She's eleven. Maurice is a very old cat. He's twenty. Twenty is really old for cats!

He's a big cat but he's thin now. He has a lovely face.

Old cats are hungry and they can eat a lot: breakfast at nine in the morning, lunch at twelve o'clock and dinner in the evening. You can give cats special milk (it's called cats' milk) but don't give them cows' milk (it's bad for them!).

He's my favorite animal because he has a great personality. He isn't very strong now but he is clever and confident. Maurice is a very special cat!

by Susie Marshall

1 Read the text. Then answer the questions.

1 What is the writer's name? ________
2 What is her friend's name? ________
3 What is the cat's name? ________
4 How old is the cat? ________
5 Is this a normal age for a cat? ________
6 Is cows' milk good for cats? ________

2 Write about your favorite animal. Use Susie's text as a model.

Introduce your animal

My favorite animal is ________.
His/Her name's ________.
He's/She's my pet/a friend's pet.

Describe your animal

He's/She's/It's ________.
(tall? thin? short? fat?)
(what color?)
And he's/she has ________.
(a tail? fur? a nice face? how many legs?)

Give instructions for the animal's care

Give him/her ________.
(How much food? How much water? Any other food or drink?)
Don't ________.

Conclusion

He's/She's my favorite animal because …

Review

1 Correct the sentences.

1 There's a milk in the fridge.
There's some milk in the fridge.
2 We have some fridge in the kitchen.
______
3 I don't have some lemonade.
______
4 There are any oranges in the cupboard.
______
5 Do you have a sugar?
______
6 The monkey has a bananas.
______
7 Janet has some waters.
______

2 Complete the conversation.

Emma Do you have [1] *any* apples?
Nigel There are [2]_______ apples in my bag.
Emma How [3]_______ apples do you have?
Nigel Four. Do you have [4]_______ lemonade?
Emma Yes, I have [5]_______ lemonade. It's here.
Nigel How [6]_______ milk do you have?
Emma Sorry. I don't have [7]_______ milk.
Nigel How about tomatoes. Do you have [8]_______ tomatoes?
Emma No. I don't have [9]_______ tomatoes.
Nigel Oh, well. We have [10]_______ apples. We can eat those.

3 Circle the correct words.

1 *Speak / Don't speak* Italian if you are in an English class.
2 If you are late for work, *run / don't run* !
3 *Use / Don't use* the computers in this room if the doors are closed.
4 If you want to eat with us, *wash / don't wash* your hands
5 *Play / Don't play* soccer here if it rains.
6 *Use / Don't use* pencil if it is the final exam. Use a pen.
7 If the kids ask, *give / don't give* candies to them. It's bad for them.
8 If you want to sleep until late tomorrow, *do / don't do* your homework tonight.

4 Unjumble the directions and instructions.

1 eb lufreca! *Be careful!*
2 tnod' urnt felt ______
3 ontd' runt thirg ______
4 og tashgrit no ______
5 post! ______
6 nurt telf ______
7 tunr ghtri ______

5 Look at the map. Write directions to get to the snakes.

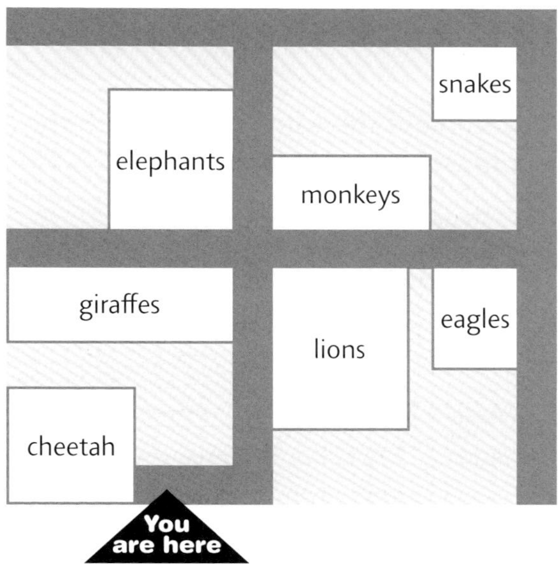

______
______
______
______
______
______
______
______

8 I hate cleaning

Presentation

1 Complete the conversation with the phrases from the box.

So where are they? No, it isn't! it smells horrible! Where's my red T-shirt? What's that?

Mark Mom! [1] *Where's my red T-shirt?*
Mom Don't shout! I always put your clean clothes on your bed.
Mark Can you see my T-shirt, Ellie?
Ellie No way! This room is a disaster area!
Mark [2] ____________
Ellie Oh, Mark! You never clean your room!
Mark Ellie, you like cleaning your room. I hate cleaning but I usually put the clean clothes near the bed.
Ellie Great! [3] ____________
Mark Umm ... maybe they're under the bed.
Ellie [4] ____________ In Clyde's basket?
Mark Hey, Ellie! Don't wake him up!
Ellie Here's your T-shirt.
Mark And my socks! Thanks Clyde.
Ellie And here's my pink top! Oh no – [5] ____________

Vocabulary

2 Write the words.

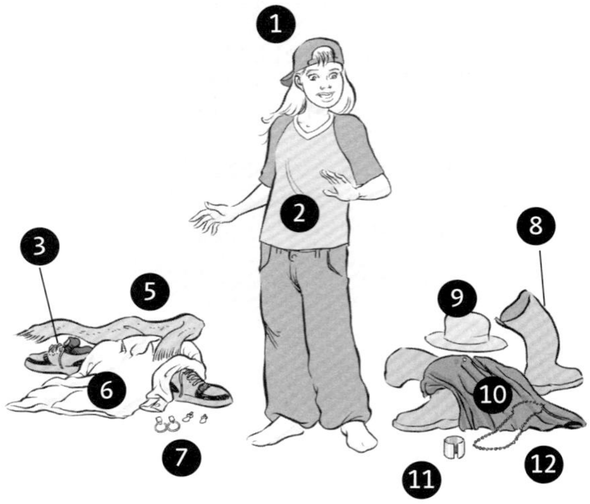

1 ____________
2 ____________
3 ____________
4 ____________
5 ____________
6 ____________
7 ____________
8 ____________
9 ____________
10 ____________
11 ____________
12 ____________

Language

Adverbs of frequency

1 Write the sentences. Put the adverbs in the correct position.

1 My brother tidies his room. (never)

2 My teacher gives me homework. (always)

3 Paula sings in a band. (sometimes)

4 I ride a bike to school. (often)

5 We wear sneakers at school. (usually)

Adverbs of frequency with *to be*

2 Write the words in the correct order.

2 he / late / usually / is

3 she / always / early / is

4 is / she / always / happy

5 never / he / friendly / is

6 never / is / happy / he

Like+ verb + *-ing*

3 Complete the sentences. Write the verbs in the correct form.

1 Do you like *getting up* (get up) early?

2 Do you like ______________ (have) breakfast?

3 Do you like ______________ (walk) to school?

4 Do you like ______________ (do) homework?

5 Do you like ______________ (sing) in the shower?

6 Do you like ______________ (listen to) the radio in the shower?

7 Do you like ______________ (go out) in the evening?

8 Do you like ______________ (dance)?

4 Answer the questions in exercise 3 about you.

All about you

1 *Yes, I like getting up early. /*
No, I don't like getting up early.

2

3

4

5

6

7

8

5 Write about your friends and your family.

Ian Jill parents grandfather brother you decide	always often usually sometimes never	play tennis go out wear party clothes ride a bike do homework clean / room use a computer you decide

1 *My grandfather often uses a computer.*

2

3

4

5

6

7

8

9

10

Language

6 Read about Tom and Jane. Match the paragraphs to the pictures.

Picture	1	2	3	4
Paragraph	*C*			

A After school, I usually wear a T-shirt, jeans and sneakers. I never wear shorts, I don't like them.

B My school uniform is a blue jacket, a grey skirt, a white shirt and a blue tie. We wear black shoes. I always wear small earrings.

C This is my favorite outfit at home – it's a black and white dress, with white boots, a white hat and white gloves. (Not really! These are clothes for a fancy dress party!)

D At school, I always wear a black jacket, grey trousers, a white shirt and a tie, and black shoes. I don't like wearing school uniform – it's horrible.

7 Answer the questions.

1 Does Jane wear school uniform?
Yes, she does.

2 How often does Tom wear uniform for school?
____

3 Does Tom like wearing his uniform?
____

4 Does Jane really wear a black-and-white dress at home?
____

5 Why doesn't Tom wear shorts?
____

8 Complete what Tom and Jane say.

Tom I usually wear a [1]__________, [2]__________ and [3]__________. I never wear [4]__________. I don't like wearing [5]__________ [6]__________.

Jane **I always wear small** [7]__________. My favorite outfit is a black and white [8]__________, with white [9]__________, a [10]__________ hat and white gloves.

9 Write the questions. Then answer them about you.

1 How often / wear / uniform ?
*How often do you wear uniform*______?
____________________.

2 Do you like / wear / sneakers ?
____________________?
____________________.

3 What / usually / wear / at home ?
____________________?
____________________.

Communicate

1 Match the words with the pictures.

a cook *8*
b clean
c do the dishes
d do the laundry
e do the shopping
f help my grandmother
g take out the trash
h make my bed
i clean my room
j look after my pet

1 
______

2 
______

3 
______

4 
______

5 
______

6 
______

7 
______

8 
a

9 
______

10 
______

2 Match the words and the faces.

1 like
2 don't like
3 love
4 don't mind
5 hate ______ (→ a)

a ☹
b 🙁
c 😐
d 🙂
e 😊

3 Look at the chart for Tom. Write the words.

Activity	Like / hate?	How often?
 1 *cooking*	🙂 *like*	50% *often*
 2 ______	☹ ______	0% ______
 3 ______	😐 ______	30% ______
 4 ______	☹ ______	100% ______

4 Write a conversation with Tom. Use the chart in exercise 3.

You *Do you like cooking* ?
Tom *Yes, I do* .
You *How often do you cook* ?
Tom *I often cook* .
You ______ ?
Tom ______ .
You ______ ?
Tom ______ .
You ______ ?
Tom ______ .
You ______ ?
Tom ______ .
You ______ ?
Tom ______ .
You ______ ?
Tom ______ .
And what do you hate doing at home?
You ______ .

Skills

1 Connect the sentences with *so*.

1 I don't have any brothers or sisters. I look after my dad.

____

2 He can't walk. He uses a wheelchair.

____

3 He's friendly and funny. I don't mind looking after him.

____

4 The club is for teenage carers. I can go there.

____

2 Write about your weekend.

Who are you?

Introduce yourself – your name, your age and where you live.

My name's ________.

What do you usually do on the weekend?

What time do you get up / go to bed?
Who do you visit?
What activities and sports do you do?
I usually get up at …

How do you help in the house?

What activities do you always / often / never do?
I hate cleaning so I never …
I usually …

Do you go out?

What do you wear?
I don't usually go out, but for a party I like wearing …

Review

1 Circle the odd ones out.

1 necklace / (jeans) / earrings
2 cap / hat / scarf
3 T-shirt / jeans / shorts
4 boots / sneakers / watch
5 top / sweatshirt / bracelet
6 socks / shirt / sandals

2 Write the adverbs.

always often never sometimes usually

100% *always*
90% ________
75% ________
50% ________
0% ________

3 Write the sentences with the adverbs in the correct position.

1 I play soccer in the afternoon. (usually)
I usually play soccer in the afternoon.
2 My family has breakfast at seven o'clock. (always)
____
3 My brother cleans his room. (never)
____
4 Steve is late for school. (sometimes)
____
5 My cat is hungry. (always)
____
6 She eats fish. (sometimes)
____
7 We walk to school. (usually)
____
8 They do their homework in the kitchen. (often)
____

4 Circle the correct verb form.

1 He likes plaing / (playing) computer games.
2 He doesn't like using / useing a cell phone.
3 She likes going / gowing out with friends.
4 We don't like reding / reading.
5 I don't like clening / cleaning my bedroom.
6 They like getting / geting up late.
7 We like watch / watching TV.

5 Write affirmative sentences (✔), negative sentences (✘) or questions (?).

1 you / like / listen to the radio ?
Do you like listening to the radio?
2 I / like / take a shower every day ✔
____
3 I / like / go to school on Monday ✘
____
4 my brother / like / play soccer ✔
____
5 he / like / walk to school ✘
____
6 you / like / wear sneakers ?
____

6 Complete the conversation with Frank.

1 **You** *Do you* like *doing* the dishes?
2 **Frank** No, I ________. I ________ it.
3 **You** How ________ do you ________ uniform?
4 **Frank** I ________ (100%) wear it.
5 **You** Do you ________ wearing uniform?
6 **Frank** Yes, I ________ it.

Review

1 Write *a*, *an* or *some*.

1 What's this? It's <u>*a*</u> chair.
2 There are _____ desks in the classroom.
3 It's _____ bed.
4 It's _____ apple.
5 I have _____ new laptop.
6 There are _____ books in my bag.
7 It's _____ sofa.
8 It's _____ large kitchen.
9 We have _____ new lamps.

2 Write *'m*, *'re* or *'s*.

1 Hello. I<u>*'m*</u> Luis.
2 This is my mother. Her name is Laura. She_____ 45.
3 This is my sister. She_____ a teacher. She_____ twenty-three.
4 This is my father. He_____ a doctor. He_____ forty-seven.
5 You_____ a student – and we_____ in the same school.

3 Write the correct form of the verb *to be*.

1 My parents <u>*are*</u> American, but I <u>*am*</u> Brazilian.
2 You _____ a good teacher.
3 It _____ my cell phone.
4 I _____ from Canada.
5 That _____ a famous picture.

4 Write *there is* or *there are*.

1 <u>*There are*</u> three rooms in my house.
2 ________ a computer in the room.
3 ________ a kitchen in the school.
4 ________ a magazine in the living room.
5 ________ six bathrooms in the school.
6 ________ thirty desks in the classroom.
7 ________ an umbrella on the sofa.

5 Write the negative form of the sentences in exercise 4.

1 <u>*There aren't*</u> three rooms in my house.
2 __________ a computer in the room.
3 __________ a kitchen in the school.
4 __________ a magazine in the living room.
5 __________ six bathrooms in the school.
6 __________ thirty desks in the classroom.
7 __________ an umbrella on the sofa.

6 Write the sentences as questions.

1 There's a cat at the window.
Is there a cat at the window?
2 There are many dogs on the street.
____
3 He has green eyes.
____
4 Felipe has a beard.
____
5 My friends have glasses.
____
6 John has long hair.
____

7 Complete the sentences with *have* or *has*.

1 They *have* big noses.
2 She _____ small hands.
3 You _____ black eyes.
4 She _____ green hair!
5 Michael _____ a mustache.
6 I _____ a big face.

8 Write negative sentences.

1 My mother has brown eyes.
My mother doesn't have brown eyes.
2 Dennis has a scar on his leg.
____
3 My teacher has short legs.
____
4 My parents have big eyes.
____
5 Cleo and Ferdinand have curly hair.
____
6 Johnson has short hair.
____

9 Find the words.

arm bathroom beard bedroom
cupboard ears foot fridge fur
hall head lamp magazine
mouth snack tail tooth umbrella

Y	D	H	H	B	K	L	D	E	T	B	M	F	E	D
I	R	E	E	T	A	B	N	M	T	J	H	R	Y	R
U	K	A	R	M	N	I	I	D	R	N	C	I	P	A
M	R	D	P	V	Z	P	Q	P	Y	A	A	D	G	O
D	O	G	T	A	Q	S	F	Y	T	L	J	G	X	B
A	O	O	G	U	M	B	R	E	L	L	A	E	H	P
H	P	A	R	W	K	B	M	P	B	O	A	M	T	U
H	M	L	T	H	K	S	B	N	E	C	C	F	O	C
A	B	R	E	B	T	H	A	S	N	K	I	G	O	M
E	L	I	A	T	E	A	R	G	L	Q	C	R	T	N
H	M	Z	S	F	K	D	B	H	O	R	P	A	G	F
H	E	R	F	O	O	T	R	J	A	T	M	L	N	H
G	A	H	T	U	O	M	R	O	P	L	T	Z	O	S
E	N	L	M	P	F	H	U	M	O	V	L	T	D	T
B	K	Q	D	J	H	Q	F	I	N	M	V	J	R	J

Review

10 Complete the sentences. Use the correct form of the verbs from the box.

cook get dressed get up meet talk walk watch

1 I like to *watch* TV before I go to bed.
2 My sister ________ before she goes to school.
3 My mom ________ very well. Her lasagna is wonderful!
4 My friend Joe and I ________ on the phone every day after school.
5 I never ________ before 6 a.m.
6 She ________ new people every day at work. She is a receptionist.
7 I ________ at the park on the weekends with my dog.

11 Complete the conversation with *do*, *does*, *don't* or *doesn't*.

Mark: Hi, Sandra. *Do* you have a minute?
Sandra: Sure. What is the problem?
Mark: I have a school project and I ________ know much about it.
Sandra: What is the project about?
Mark: Contemporary art. My teacher wants a poster for Monday.
Sandra: ________ she want a collage or text?
Mark: We can choose. But she ________ want anything copied from the internet.
Sandra: Of course not. ________ you have any ideas?
Mark: No, I ________. Do you think a collage is a good idea?
Sandra: Yes, I have some art magazines at home. We can look for some cool images.
Mark: Great!

12 Look at Pete's appointment book and answer the questions.

Monday	Tuesday	Wednesday
dentist at 10 A.M.	soccer game at 9 P.M.	research at library from 12 to 4 P.M.

Thursday	Friday	Saturday	Sunday
English classes from 7 to 9 P.M.	cook dinner for friends	swim at the club from 7 to 8 A.M.	run at the park in the morning

1 It is Tuesday, 9 P.M. What is Pete doing?
He is playing soccer.
2 Can Pete go to the movies on Thursday at 8 P.M.? Why?
____
3 It is Friday night. What is Pete doing?
____
4 Can Pete use a cell phone at the library?
____
5 Can Pete swim?
____

13 Look at the clocks and complete the dialogs.

1
A: What time is it?
B: *It's ten.*
A: What are you doing?
B: ____________________ (homework)
A: Can you come out and play?
B: ____________________ (✗)

2
A: What time is it?
B: ____________________
A: What are you doing?
B: ____________________ (read/book)
A: Can you help me with my homework?
B: ____________________ (✓)

3
A: What time is it?
B: ____________________
A: What are you doing?
B: ____________________ (lunch)
A: Can you play video games with me?
B: ____________________ (✓)

4
A: What time is it?
B: ____________________
A: What are you doing?
B: ____________________ (surf/internet)
A: Can you upload some photos?
B: ____________________ My USB port is not working. (✗)

5
A: What time is it?
B: ____________________
A: What are you doing?
B: ____________________ (go/bed)
A: Can you play video games now?
B: ____________________ I have to get up early tomorrow. (✗)

6
A: What time is it?
B: ____________________
A: What are you doing?
B: ____________________ (movie)
A: Can I watch the movie with you?
B: ____________________ Come here. (✓)

14 Write the negative and interrogative form of these sentences.

1 She is speaking English with her teacher.
She isn't speaking English with her teacher.
Is she speaking English with her teacher?

2 We can play soccer after class.
____
____

3 Eric lives in an apartment.
____
____

4 Susan and Michael study with me.
____
____

5 Karate is a violent sport.
____
____

Review

15 Write the words from the box under the right column.

art boots bracelet cap chicken cow duck earrings elephant furniture gas goldfish hat information love money music scarf skirt snake socks sugar water

Countable nouns	Uncountable nouns
boots	

16 Choose the correct answer.

1 My mother needs ***some/any*** apples for a pie.
2 You can't see **some/any** fishes in the tank. The water is too dirty.
3 We don't have **some/any** oil in the house.
4 Rick doesn't read **some/any** books about war.
5 He always puts ***some/any*** milk with his coffee.
6 I have ***some/any*** old comic books.
7 There aren't **some/any** lions at the zoo.
8 They have ***some/any*** interesting photos of the city.

17 Write *much* or *many* and answer the questions.

1 How *many* students are there in your class?
______
2 How ______ dogs are there in your house?
______
3 How ______ money do you have with you now?
______
4 How ______ water do you drink every day?
______

18 Use the words from the box to complete the sentences. Make any necessary adjustments.

get are work drive ask come

1 If my father drinks, he never *drives*.
2 If I am lost, I always ______ for directions.
3 If I don't sleep well, I don't ______ well.
4 If you press EJECT, the CD ______ out.
5 If you mix red and yellow, you ______ orange.
6 If you are born in Rome, you ______ Italian.

19 Look at the information below and complete the sentences with *always*, *often*, *never*, *sometimes* or *usually*.

ACTIVITY	Mon	Tue	Wed	Thu	Fri	Sat	Sun
wear uniform to go to school	✔	✔	✔	✔	✔		
read news online		✔		✔		✔	
update my blog	✔		✔		✔		✔
late for school							
do the shopping for my mom				✔			

Hi, my name is Adam. I'm twelve. I study at St. George High in Florida. I really like it and I'm *never* late for school. I _________ wear a uniform to go to school, but it's OK. My uniform is nice.
After school I like to read or surf the internet. I _________ read news online, specially about sports. I _________ update my blog, there are many interesting things to post.
I help my mother too. I clean my bedroom every day and I _________ do the shopping for my mom.
What about you?

20 Choose the right option.

1 I love ***cook/cooking*** but I usually ***cook/cooking*** with my mother's help.
2 I like ***do/doing*** homework with my friends. We sometimes ***do/doing*** homework at the school library.
3 I don't mind ***clean/cleaning*** my room, but I never ***clean/cleaning*** it on Sundays.
4 I don't like ***wear/wearing*** uniforms, but students ***wear/wearing*** uniforms in my school.
5 I ***drink/drinking*** milk every morning, because the doctor recommended. But I hate ***drink/drinking*** it!

21 Write the sentences in the correct order.

1 is / for / never / work / late / she /.
She is never late for work.
2 I / surf / often / internet / the /.
____
3 sometimes / our / is / mess / a / bedroom /.
____
4 always / I / to / go / bed / 11p.m. / before /.
____
5 she / usually / for / has / breakfast / cereal /.
____
6 is / school / Peter / at / this / at / often / time /.
____
7 go / to / I / don't / park / Mondays / the / on / normally /.
____
8 is / my / happy / always / teacher /.
____
9 forget / homework / sometimes / my / I /.
____
10 winter / swim / the / I / in / never / .
____

Wordlist

Starter 1

1–100
bag
bee
black
blue
board
book
brown
car
color
eye
go
green
how do you spell?
it's
name
notebook
orange (adj)
pencil
pencil case
poster
red
student
table
teacher
white
yellow
your

Starter 2

am
are
computer
dad
friend
from
he
hello
hi
I
it
is
mom
my
she
sister
that
this

Unit 1

Lesson 1

cat
dog
DVD
excuse me
family
football
how old
orange (n)
pizza
please
problem
radio
TV
umbrella
where

Lesson 2

first
her
his
house
its

Lesson 3

brother
good afternoon
good evening
good morning
month
twin

Lesson 4

baseball
best friend
cap
class
cool
favorite thing
glove
home
new
nice
now
old
picture
popular
present
really
school
sport
team

Unit 2

Lesson 1

bike
but
English
hat
key
know
magazine
pen
shoe
too
wallet
watch (n)
we

Lesson 2

actor
animal
film
girlfriend
our
Scottish
they

Lesson 3

American
be
British
China
Chinese
France
French
Greece
Greek
Italian
Italy
Poland
Polish
Portugal
Portuguese
Russia
Russian
sorry
Spain
Spanish
The USA
Turkey
Turkish

Lesson 4

big
club
holiday
lucky

Unit 3

Lesson 1

bathroom
bed
bedroom
behind
Boo!
box
bug
Come on!
cooker
cupboard
desk
dining room
door
fridge
hall
in front of
kitchen
lamp
locked
next to
room
scared
living room
sofa
there
under
upstairs

Lesson 2

clothes
floor
map
window

Lesson 3

aunt
cousin
daughter
girl
granddad
granddaughter
grandfather
grandmother
grandson
husband
nephew
niece
son
uncle
wife

Lesson 4

college
different
full name
jigsaw
penfriend
place

Unit 4

Lesson 1

arm
bald
beard
blond
character
costume
curly
ears
face
foot
funny
fur
hair
hand
head
horrible
leg
long
man
mirror
mustach
mouth
nose
ready
reflection
scar
short
straight
tail
tooth
ugly

Lesson 2

bank robbery
description
gold
intelligent
police
search for
today

Lesson 3
beautiful
clever
confident
fat
friendly
shy
strong
tall
thin
weak
young

Lesson 4
brave
donkey
great
princess
small

Unit 5

Lesson 1
be careful
cook
egg
fast
guitar
horse
hungry
juggle
omelete
onion
safe
sound
speak
swim
take (it) off
tomato
use

Lesson 2
become
body
fly
invisible
stretch
through
ton
wall

Lesson 3
apple
baked potato
banana
beans
burgers
certainly
cheese
chicken
chips
customer
fabulous
fairground
fine
fish (n)
motorcycle
pasta
peach
pear
peas
salad
waiter

Lesson 4
after
competition
electric
kid
last
musician
ordinary
rock music
show (n)
stage
talented
tonight
violin
weird
winner

Unit 6

Lesson 1
any
camera
cow
cute
duck
eagle
elephant
farm
food
giraffe
give
goldfish
lion
monkey
peanut
rabbit
shout
silly
snake
some
tree

Lesson 2
cake
sugar

Lesson 3
buy
do homework
eat
left
right
sandwich
talk
text (v)
turn
walk
wash

Lesson 4
because
blind
cheetah
crocodile
flash
go back
guide
harness
instructions
reports
see
simple
take a photo
touch
understand

Unit 7

Lesson 1
breakfast
computer game
dinner
get dressed
job
lunch
shower
spy
sunglasses
think
time
visit
work

Lesson 2
late
newspaper
sleep
us
weekend

Lesson 3
calendar
count
day
Friday
help
letter
Monday
o'clock
read
Saturday
Sunday
them
Thursday
Tuesday
Wednesday
write
Lesson 4
activity
bacon
beach

camp
campfire
cereal
clean
fruit
learn
picnic
play cards
rest
scary
sing
story
tell
tennis
volleyball
wake

Unit 8

Lesson 1
always
basket
boots
bracelet
dress
earring
jacket
jeans
necklace
put
sandals
scarf
shirt
shorts
skirt
smell
socks
sweatshirt
top
T-shirt

Lesson 2
full
uniform
usually
wear

Lesson 3
cold
don't mind
do the shopping
look after
love
meet
take out

Lesson 4
adult
boring
earn
expensive
fun
hour
live (v)
lonely
model
session
slogan
studio
teenage
travel
wool

PEARSON

Diretor editorial e de conteúdo Roger Trimer
Gerente editorial Kelly Tavares
Coordenadora editorial Veronica Teodorov
Editor de desenvolvimento Renato Vieira Malkov
Editor assistente Mauricio Shiroma
Editor de campo Allan Cravo
Editora de mídia e desenvolvimento Mirian Navarro
Editor de produção Gustavo Reis
Assistente de arte Lucas Medeiros
Assistente editorial Carolina Bostigo
Editora de iconografia Maiti Salla
Assistente de iconografia e licenciamento de texto Cristiane Gameiro
Adaptação de projeto gráfico Gustavo Reis
Capa Lucas Medeiros
Editoração eletrônica Figurattiva Editorial
Ilustrações Kleber Moraes, Estúdio Mil e Estúdio Ornitorrinco
Produção de áudio Maximal Studio
Manual do professor Jenny Parsons

Créditos das imagens: p. 4 A Gareth Boden, B Pearson Education Ltd:, C Gareth Boden; p. 5 Kobal Collection Ltd: Walt Disney; p. 7 A vectorlib.com / Shutterstock, B Monika Hunackova / Shutterstock, C kanate / Shutterstock, D VooDoo13 / Shutterstock, E SlipFloat / Shutterstock, F sonia.eps / Shutterstock; p. 8 A Fedor Selivanov / Shutterstock, B Maxisport / Shutterstock; p. 9 A Valentina Razumova / Shutterstock, B Vasilius / Shutterstock, C Sergej Razvodovskij / Shutterstock, D Edhar / Shutterstock, E gyn9037 / Shutterstock, F Mike Flippo / Shutterstock, G Paul_Brighton / Shutterstock, H Arunas Gabalis / Shutterstock, I Trinochka / Shutterstock; p. 10 A Getty Images: Jean Ayissi / AFP, B, C Corbis: Mario Anzuoni / Reuters, D Haider Sahah /AFP; p. 11 Andresr / Shutterstock; p. 12 A PhotoStock10 / Shutterstock, B Dmitry Lobanov / Shutterstock, C studioVin / Shutterstock, D Marine's / Shutterstock; p. 13 A Tribalium / Shutterstock, B lugyana / Shutterstock, C Matthew Cole / Shutterstock, D enterlinedesign / Shutterstock, E JSDgraphics / Shutterstock, F Rocket400 Studio / Shutterstock, G Nikiparonak / Shutterstock, H notkoo / Shutterstock, I Vadelma / Shutterstock, J bayberry / Shutterstock; p. 14 A PhotoEdit Inc.: David Young Wolff, B HomeStudio / Shutterstock, C Songquan Deng / Shutterstock, D eddtoro / Shutterstock, E Songquan Deng / Shutterstock, F SeanPavonePhoto / Shutterstock; p. 18 Pearson Education Ltd: Gareth Boden; p. 20 Pearson Education Ltd: Gareth Boden; p. 22 Pearson Education Ltd: Gareth Boden; p. 23 Corbis: @Chris Carroll; p. 24 A Saul Loeb / AFP, B Pete Souza/ AFP, C Chip Somodevilla / Getty Images / AFP, D Mandel NGAN / AFP, E Mandel NGAN / AFP; p. 28 Pearson Education Ltd: Gareth Boden; p. 32 Rex Features: ABC / Everett , B Aquarius Collection: 20th Century Fox, C Kobal Collection Ltd: Universal / bruce McBroom; p. 38 Lasse Kristensen / Shutterstock; p. 40 A Getty Images: Jeffry Bosdet / All Canada Photos, Masterfile UK Ltd: Jerzyworks; p. 42 Pearson Education Ltd: Gareth Boden; p. 47 Imaginechina / AFP; p. 48 Monkey Business / Thinkstock ; p. 49 A iStockphoto: digital planet design, B Photofusion Pictures Library: Digital Nation, C Creatas Images, D Jupter Unlimited: BananaStock , E Comstock Images, F Brand X Pictures , G Corbis: Tara Moore / zefa , H Butch Martin / Photographer's Choice , I Rex Features: Dimitis Legakis , J Herb Schmitz , K M Morgan Photography , L Getty Images: peter Dazeley / Photographer's Choice , M Bob Thomas / Stone ; p. 52 A Muellek Josef / Shutterstock, B SergiyN / Shutterstock, C Fuse / Getty Images, D Fotokostic / Shutterstock, E Dennis Galante / Stone+ / Getty Images, F Goodluz / Shutterstock; p. 53 Pearson Education Ltd: Gareth Boden; p. 54 iStockphoto: 3alexd; p. 55 A Getty Images: Jan Sonnenmair / Aurora, B Corbis> Graham West / zefa ; p. 58 Pearson Education Ltd: Gareth Boden; p. 63 Pearson Education Ltd: Gareth Boden; p. 64 Photolibrary.com: Stefan Berg / Johner; p. 67 A Nitr / Shutterstock, B mama_mia / Shutterstock, C Brian A Jackson / Shutterstock, D BW Folsom / Shutterstock, E duckeesue / Shutterstock; p. 68 Pearson Education Ltd: Gareth Boden; p.69 A Skynesher, B Corbis Arthur Morris, C Herbert Spichtinger / zefa , D Jupiter Unlimited: BananaStock, E Thinkstock Images, F Sleeve, G iStockphoto: Digital Build, H Josh Lewis Photography, I Serega, J Photolibrary.com: Bates Littlehates / Animals Animals, K Photos.com, L Mike Rega, M Global Photographer, N Sirius_r, O jcyoung2 ; p. 72 Divulgação / U.S. Department of Homeland and Security; p. 74 A iStockphoto: bobbymn, B Photolibrary.com: Mike Mcgill / Flirt Collection ; p. 75 Alamy Images: Rudi Theunis; p. 78 Pearson Education Ltd: Gareth Boden; p. 80 iStockphoto / Thinkstock; p. 81 Jupter Unlimited: BananaStock; p. 82 A Pearson Education Ltd:, B Gareth Boden ; p. 84 A Alamy Images: Andrew Peterson , B Getty Images: Charley Gallay; p. 85 Corbis: ©Michelle Pedone / zefa; p. 87 A Miera / Shutterstock, B dboystudio / Shutterstock, C B-C Images / Getty Images, D dboystudio / Shutterstock.

Dados Internacionais de Catalogação na Publicação (CIP)
(Câmara Brasileira do Livro, SP, Brasil)

Rose, Jim
Forward! : student book, 2 / Jim Rose...[et al.]. -- 1. ed. -- São Paulo : Pearson Education do Brasil, 2014.
Outros autores: Steve Elsworth, Ron Martinez, Candy Martinez
ISBN 978-85-8143-815-3
1. Inglês (Ensino médio) I. Rose, Jim. II. Elsworth, Steve. III. Martinez, Ron. IV. Martinez, Candy.
13-08073 CDD-420.7

Índices para catálogo sistemático:
1. Inglês : Ensino médio 420.7

ISBN 978-85-8143-815-3 Forward 2 Student Book
ISBN 978-85-8143-929-7 Forward 2 Student Book with MyLab
ISBN 978-85-4300-048-0 Forward 2 Student Book with eText
ISBN 978-85-8143-826-9 Forward 2 Teacher Book

Pearson Education do Brasil Ltda.,
uma empresa do grupo Pearson Education
Avenida Santa Marina, 1193 – CEP: 05036-001 – São Paulo, SP – Brasil